ON THE TREE OF THE CROSS

Georges Florovsky and the Patristic Doctrine of Atonement

On the Tree of the Cross

Georges Florovsky and the Patristic Doctrine of Atonement

Edited by

Matthew Baker, Seraphim Danckaert,
and Nicholas Marinides

HOLY TRINITY SEMINARY PRESS
HOLY TRINITY PUBLICATIONS
Holy Trinity Monastery
Jordanville, New York

Printed with the blessing of His Eminence,
Metropolitan Hilarion First Hierarch
of the Russian Orthodox Church Outside of Russia

Anthology:
On the Tree of the Cross,
Georges Florovsky and the Patristic Doctrine of Atonement
© 2016 Holy Trinity Monastery

HOLY TRINITY
SEMINARY PRESS

An imprint of

HOLY TRINITY PUBLICATIONS
Holy Trinity Monastery
Jordanville, New York 13361-0036
www.holytrinitypublications.com

ISBN: 978–1-942699–28-6 (paperback)
ISBN: 978–1-942699–09-5 (hardback)
ISBN: 978–1-942699-13-2 (ePub)
ISBN: 978–1-942699-14-9 (Mobipocket)

Library of Congress Control Number: 2016935423

Dedication

To Fr Georges, ἡ πάντων ἡμῶν ἀκόνη

and to

Fr Paul Schafran, Andrew Blane, and Alexis Klimoff,

witnesses to his legacy

and in memory of our beloved brother

Fr Matthew Baker (1977–2015)

τελευτήσαντος ἀνδρὸς δικαίου οὐκ ὄλλυται ἐλπίς

UNIVERSITY OF LONDON

SPECIAL UNIVERSITY LECTURES IN

THEOLOGY

A COURSE OF THREE LECTURES

ON

"PATRISTIC DOCTRINE OF ATONEMENT"

WILL BE GIVEN AT

~~KING'S COLLEGE, LONDON~~

(STRAND, W.C. 2)

BY

The Rev. Prof. GEORGE FLOROVSKY

(Professor in the Orthodox Theological Institute, Paris)

at 5.30 p.m. on

NOVEMBER 5th, 10th and 12th, 1936

SYLLABUS

LECTURE I.—*Agnus Dei.*—Incarnation and Sacrifice. How could the Incarnate die? The Original Sin and Death universal. The healing of human nature.

LECTURE II.—*Triduum mortis.*—High-Priest and Victim. Sacrifice and Mystery. The Last Supper and Calvary. Christ's Death as a Victory. The Glory of the Resurrection.

LECTURE III.—*Totus Christus, caput et corpus.*—Sacraments and Ascesis. "Death in Christ" and "Life in Spirit." The Holy Baptism. The Eucharistic Sacrifice and Mystery. "Una Sancta. . ."

At the First Lecture the Chair will be taken by

The Rev. Prof. H. MAURICE RELTON, D.D.

(Professor of Biblical and Historical Theology in the University)

The Lectures are addressed to students of the University and to others interested in the subject.

ADMISSION FREE, WITHOUT TICKET

S. J. WORSLEY,
Academic Registrar.

540/4/500/1-9-36/C.P. 13580

The original flyer announcing Florovsky's lectures on "The Patristic Doctrine of Atonement," given at King's College, London in November 1936.

Unprocessed Papers (teaching and writing material); dates not examined; Georges Florovsky Papers (C0586)
Box 10, Manuscripts Division, Department of Rare Books and Special Collections, Princeton University Library.

Contents

✠

Preface

THE PRESENT VOLUME IS COMPOSED of two parts. The first is a collection of papers, originally delivered at the first annual patristic symposium in honor of Fr Georges Florovsky at Princeton University and Princeton Theological Seminary on February 11–12, 2011. The second part is a collection of writings on atonement by Fr Florovsky himself, taken from several unpublished manuscripts as well as published works which have never been reprinted or translated. Both parts of the volume have their own introductions, with information about the provenance of the previously unpublished manuscripts and their editing in the introduction to the second part.

A few words about the doctrine of atonement in the present-day context are necessary, particularly as the concept has not received sufficient attention in Orthodox circles since the suggestive work of Fr Florovsky. In fact, some recent Orthodox theologians have tended to paint all "Western" treatments of redemption with a very broad brush, only to dismiss them as something altogether foreign to the patristic and Orthodox tradition. Yet it should not be necessary to point out the obvious: theologians as diverse as Augustine, Anslem, Aquinas, Calvin, Barth, and Balthasar are not all saying the same thing. Nor is the notion of an atoning "substitution" or vicarious representation—motifs not altogether lacking in the Greek Fathers—reducible merely to the strictly "forensic" framework often decried by Orthodox theologians and certainly not to the penal model unique to certain Reformed traditions. Such was true in previous ages and is even more the case today. Indeed, in modern theological discourse, the diversity of atonement theories is starkly apparent.

Within this pluralistic and polarized context, the need for an authentic and informed Orthodox voice is all the more pressing. Yet in making such a voice articulate we must first realize that the critique of a one-sidedly juridical view of atonement is not something at all unique to the Orthodox East. For just as Orthodox theologians over the last century had begun to question the theology of redemption that had become common during the centuries of "Latin captivity" diagnosed and critiqued by Florovsky, Roman Catholic and Protestant theologians were beginning to do the same, highlighting and embracing

9

more holistic approaches to be found in both patristic and post-schism Western sources. Thus, the situation is now much changed from what it was a century ago. The picture presented by the official *Catechism of the Catholic Church*, published in 1997 and reflecting the fruits of the mid-century patristic *ressourcement*, is rather different and considerably broader than what we find in the Decrees of the Council of Trent or reflected in the neo-scholastic theology and popular piety of the Roman Catholic Church a hundred years ago. Likewise, the atonement theology of such major recent Reformed theologians as T.F. Torrance and Colin Gunton is a far cry from that of the Westminster Confession or the Princeton theologians of the 19th and early 20th centuries.

In view of such developments, those Orthodox concerned with distinguishing the Orthodox teaching from erroneous or imbalanced understandings of the doctrine of redemption must be especially careful not to engage in shadow-boxing with opponents who are no longer present. New challenges call for a response. In recent years, the pendulum has shifted considerably among various Western confessions and their academic theological representatives towards an outright rejection of *any* idea of requisite sacrifice or divinely willed atonement for sin. Some recent feminist theologians, mirroring an extreme version of penal atonement propagated by certain strands of hyper-Reformed orthodoxy, have come to characterize any notion that the death of Christ is an atoning sacrificial oblation as a form of "divine child abuse"—one which would underwrite and justify the further abuse of other human beings. Apparently, what is needed is not atonement, but liberation: a political liberation that we ourselves should effect through our own revolutionary social efforts.

Ironically, the staunchly categorical aversion to the idea of "atonement" on the part of some Orthodox theologians—often those most critical of the Christian West—dovetails, in certain respects, if not with such radical secularization of the message of redemption, then at least with certain more liberal tendencies within the Western theological establishment. In more moderate quarters, one hears an appeal to the theology of deification as if it were a kind of alternative soteriological "model," opposed and in contradistinction to the idea of Christ's vicarious offering in atonement for sin. Yet the fact remains: the language of vicarious representation, sacrifice, and legal vindication used to describe various facets of the saving work of Jesus Christ is to be found both in the Bible and the Fathers, where it has crucial and abiding theological significance. What the language of atonement indicates is not an alternative "model" to *theosis*, but rather a crucial dimension of that multi-faceted plan of the Creator to save His fallen creatures from death and destruction and to raise them up into union with Him.

While affirming deification as the original plan of the Creator God and as the goal of Christian life, Orthodox theologians today must also maintain the objective reality of the divine and atoning acts accomplished historically once and for all on our behalf, without which the ultimate end of union with God would be impossible for fallen human beings. The Church's sacramental and ascetical life allows us to hold these tensions together: it presumes the objective reality of the victory won on the Cross and of the continuing high priestly ministry of the ascended Jesus, while also inviting us to a free and active personal participation in these realities.

It is here that we Orthodox, attempting to take the full measure of our historic tradition, can indeed provide an important corrective. It must first of all be said that the Orthodox Church has ever maintained the Christology of the great Ecumenical Councils at the forefront of her theological consciousness, even at the most popular level. Indeed, it is the Orthodox alone who celebrate liturgically the commemoration of the Fathers of the Councils collectively as such. Historically much more reticent than the various Western confessions to commit herself to any particular soteriological "theory," the Orthodox tradition has maintained a deep-seated awareness that it is the doctrine of the *person* of Christ that provides the key to apprehending the pattern and the unity of God's redemptive *work*.

Further, the Orthodox Church is, if nothing else, a liturgical church, with a theology deeply informed by the experience of liturgical worship. It is good to be reminded that the very notion of "atonement" in the Christian tradition has its distant origin in a liturgical context—in the Temple liturgy of *Yom Kippur,* the Day of Atonement. The liturgical aspect evident here persists throughout the scriptural witness. The main soteriological metaphor in the Epistle to the Hebrews is thoroughly liturgical. Indeed, a number of Western scholars have themselves recently concluded that the substitutionary language found throughout the Pauline corpus is often more liturgical than legal. It is therefore hardly surprising that the witness of the Fathers and the experience of the Orthodox liturgy remind us that atonement is, above all, a liturgical act, the sacrifice being not only a death but also ascension and glorification. It is as "apostle and high priest of our confession" (Heb 3:1)—the *Schaliach* sent from God with the blessing of peace, the priest chosen from among men to make sacrifices and intercessions on behalf of his brethren—that Jesus undertakes the work of atonement, "ministering the things of God to us, and ours to God".[1] In the Old Covenant, the high priest entered the Holy of Holies once a year, on

---

[1]([Ps.-]Athanasius, *Oratio IV Contra Arianos*, PG 26: 476B).

the Day of Atonement. So likewise, our high priest has entered the heavenly sanctuary still bearing our humanity in Himself, bringing our names into continual remembrance before God, bearing us upon His heart, offering the whole creation to God. As St. Gregory the Theologian confesses: "For He pleads even now as man for my salvation, for he continues to be with the body which He assumed".[2] It is into this heavenly liturgy, which Christ performs before the face of the Father, the re-presentation of His sacrifice on our behalf, that the Church is drawn in her worship. It is Jesus Himself who, upon His ascension in glory, is the one chief "liturgist of the sanctuary" (Heb 8:2), the "bishop of our souls" (1 Pet 2:25), and "the Amen, the faithful and true witness" (Rev 3:14), who "ever liveth to make intercession for us" (Heb 7:25) and through whom we offer our *Amen* to God (2 Cor 1:20). True God, worshiped with the Father and the Spirit, Christ Jesus also "worships with us as man . . . both offering himself as for a fragrant scent on our behalf, and us through himself and in himself to God the Father".[3]

With all these themes in mind, the present volume attempts to examine the doctrine of atonement with renewed vigor and faithfulness. Its contents are not uniform, nor do they pretend to be comprehensive. A fuller exploration ought to have included chapters on the Epistle to the Hebrews and the Pauline literature, St Cyril of Alexandria, the important but sorely neglected atonement theology of Nicholas of Methone and the local Council of Constantinople convened in 1157 (the decrees of which are reflected in the Synodikon of Orthodoxy), the thought of St Nicholas Cabasilas, and perhaps a number of more recent Orthodox authorities. There is also an urgent need for greater Orthodox theological engagement with those pre-schism Latin authorities who are acknowledged Fathers and ecumenical teachers for the Orthodox as well. Taken as a whole, however, the essays in part one of the present collection, as well as the suggestive samples of Fr Florovsky's own writings in part two, represent a first and significant step toward advancing one of Florovsky's life-long goals: to clarify and promulgate the Orthodox teaching on atonement, drawing from the witness of the Holy Fathers in the context of a sincere dialogue with non-Orthodox Christians.

We wish to offer profound thanks to friends and colleagues in the Fr Georges Florovsky Orthodox Christian Theological Society at Princeton University and the School of Christian Vocation and Mission at Princeton Theological Seminary, the two entities that organized the original symposium; and also to the

---

[2] (*Oratio XXX* 14, PG 36: 121C).
[3] (Cyril of Alexandria, *Adversus Nestorium*, PG 76: 116AB).

symposium's many financial sponsors, including Princeton University's Gradu-ate Student Events Board, Seeger Center for Hellenic Studies, Department of History, Council on the Humanities, Office of Religious Life, and Orthodox Christian Fellowship. Special thanks also belong to Andrew Blane, whose care for Florovsky's legacy is only equaled by his magnanimous desire to see it con-tinue, and to Presvytera Katherine Baker for permission to publish certain items in part two of this volume. Finally, our gratitude goes to those who supported various aspects of the editing process, including the Fellowship of St Alban and St Sergius in Oxford and the Office of Vocation and Ministry at Hellenic College, to David Heith-Stade for translating one of Florovsky's articles from Swedish, and to Jeremy David Wallace and Eugenia Torrance for their editorial help, particularly in undertaking the tedious task of transcribing Florovsky's manuscripts.

M. Baker, S. Danckaert, N. Marinides
Princeton, NJ

Abbreviations

ACCS	Ancient Christian Commentary on Scripture (ed. Thomas Oden; Downer's Grove, Ill.: InterVarsity Press, 1998–)
ANF	Ante-Nicene Fathers (Buffalo: Christian Literature Company, 1885–1896; repr. Grand Rapids: Eerdmans, 1987)
GOTR	*Greek Orthodox Theological Review*
JBL	*Journal of Biblical Literature*
OCP	*Orientalia Christiana Periodica*
PG	Patrologiae Cursus Completus, Series Graeca (ed. Jacques Paul Migne; Paris: Imprimerie Catholique, 1857–1866)
PL	Patrologiae Cursus Completus, Series Latina (ed. Jacques Paul Migne; Paris: Imprimerie Catholique, 1841–1855)
"Redemption"	Georges Florovsky, "Redemption," in *Creation and Redemption* (vol. 3 of *Collected works of Georges Florovsky*; Belmont, Mass.: Nordland, 1976), 95–162, 280–309.
SC	Sources Chrétiennes (Paris: Les Editions du Cerf, 1942–)
SJT	*Scottish Journal of Theology*
SVSQ	*St Vladimir's Seminary Quarterly*
SVTQ	*St. Vladimir's Theological Quarterly*
WUNT	Wissenschaftliche Untersuchungen zum Neuen Testament (Tübingen: Mohr Siebeck, 1950–)

PART I

PROCEEDINGS OF THE SYMPOSIUM

Introduction
Marcus Plested

Thou hast redeemed us from the curse of the Law by Thy precious Blood. By being nailed to the Cross and pierced with the Spear, Thou hast poured immortality on mankind. O our Saviour, glory to Thee.

(Orthodox Troparion for Good Friday)

Upon the Altar of the Cross / His Body hath redeemed our loss:/ and tasting of His roseate Blood, / our life is hid with Him in God.

(Ancient Latin Hymn for Eastertide)

"ATONEMENT" HAS THE DISTINCTION of being virtually the only theological term of wholly English origin. Used by Tyndale to render the Greek καταλλαγή (reconciliation), atonement speaks first and foremost of the "at-one-ing" of God and man, the reestablishment through the saving work of Christ of the union and communion lost at the Fall. Only secondarily has the term become overlaid with notions of expiation, propitiation, sacrifice, and substitution—associations that have made many Orthodox theologians instinctively uncomfortable with the term. Modern Orthodox soteriology has, very broadly speaking, tended to privilege the cosmic themes of creation, incarnation, and deification over the historical drama of fall and redemption, themes that have typically received greater attention in the Christian West. The experience of the divine light can be a more familiar topic for many Orthodox than the atoning death of Christ, the transfiguration a more congenial subject than the crucifixion, deification a more enticing prospect than mere redemption from sin. But the theological vision of Fr Georges Florovsky is one that adroitly encompasses all these necessary dimensions of Christian faith and that militates strongly against any sort of simplistic East-West dichotomy.

Florovsky is indeed one of the few writers in either East or West able to unite so cogently the themes of creation and fall, incarnation and atonement, and deification and redemption. This quality of balance is very much the product of his immersion in the Fathers of East and West alike. Florovsky's theological program was consciously catholic in its deliberate encompassing of both Latin and Greek patristic traditions with all their distinctive emphases and insights. Florovsky's whole conception of a neopatristic synthesis, let us recall, is posited on the underlying harmony of these traditions. The ubiquitous references in his works to Latin teachers, theological terms, and liturgical texts eloquently proclaim his conviction of the essential unity of East and West. It is no accident that he should have chosen to devote particular attention to the atonement—a theme that has historically preoccupied the West to a greater extent than it has the East. Indeed Florovsky's essay on the atonement may be considered the closest he ever came to producing a tangible example of neopatristic synthesis in practice.

The essay "*In Ligno Crucis*: The Patristic Doctrine of the Atonement" presents itself as a "positive reconstruction of the original patristic doctrine." This "systematic reconstruction" is offered as proof "that just by return to the Fathers one may regain a solid basis for theological research" and a "pointer toward what one may describe as a *neopatristic synthesis*." In affirming the ongoing relevance, vitality, and richness of the patristic tradition, he appeals to Louis Thomassin's declamation, "*Inexhaustum est penu theologiae patrum*" ("the storehouse of the theology of the Fathers is inexhaustible"). The fact that a seventeenth-century Catholic theologian should figure so prominently in Florovsky's single most programmatic statement as to the nature of his envisaged neo-patristic synthesis speaks volumes as to the properly catholic nature of that undertaking.

Florovsky's hope that his work on the patristic doctrine of the atonement would stimulate further research has been amply borne out by the papers presented in this volume. One of his favorite reference points was, as we have mentioned, the Latin liturgy. The very title of his essay on atonement, "*in ligno crucis*" ("on the wood of the Cross") takes us back to the Latin liturgy for the exaltation of the Cross. Another favored phrase used by Fr Florovksy, "*in ara crucis*" ("on the altar of the Cross") comes from the Ambrosian hymn cited above. Fr Irenei Steenberg rightly homes in on the dimension of liturgy in his "A Sacrifice for Life: Atonement in the Orthodox Liturgical Tradition." While the emphasis here is on the Orthodox as opposed to the Latin liturgy (and to the eucharistic liturgy in particular), his intuition as to the indispensability of the liturgical matrix is certainly congruent with that of Fr Florovsky. Perhaps the most arresting assertion in this paper is that "the synthesis of the Fathers is the Divine Liturgy of the Church." As "mouthpieces for the Church's liturgical revelation of the Kingdom," the Fathers voice a united witness to the same liturgical experience. As a devout admirer of St Augustine, Fr Florovsky may have been pleased to see in this paper a sophisticated vindication of that ardent

Augustinian, Prosper of Aquitaine, in his famous declaration that the *lex orandi*, the rule of prayer, establishes the *lex credendi*, the rule of faith.

Moving on now to some of the specifics of the patristic teaching(s) on the atonement, Fr John Behr presents us with a *tour de force* entitled "Irenaeus on 'Atonement'." While rightly suspicious of any artificial compartmentalization or systematization, Behr presents us with a profound set of insights into St Irenaeus' comprehensive and coherent account of the mystery of redemption. Behr emphasizes the interconnectedness and inseparability of incarnation and atonement, deftly doing away with any hint that the incarnation was merely God's Plan B after Adam and Eve had wrecked Plan A. The paper is especially penetrating when it comes to the matter of death: "Death is a catastrophe—we should weep and wail; but, it is also a marvel, a miracle, a mystery (a "sacrament")—to which we have been wedded by the command of God, no less." These two aspects of the same reality depend very much on perspective. The same may be said of Christ's work of salvation—freeing from sin *and* bestowing immortality. As in the troparion for Good Friday, quoted at the beginning of this introduction, these actions are to be recognized as two dimensions of one and the same eternal economy of salvation.

Fr Khaled Anatolios's paper delves further into the patristic treasury through a close and exacting reading of a theologian whom Florovsky regarded as of quite decisive importance in regard to the theme of atonement–St Athanasius of Alexandria. Perhaps the most distinctive feature of this paper is its compelling argument for the correlation of the doctrines of creation and redemption in Athanasius. Basing himself on Athanasius' master work, the double treatise *Against the Pagans – On the Incarnation*, Anatolios comprehensively undermines the false dichotomy between 'ontological' and 'juridical' accounts of salvation that is sometimes assumed to obtain between Greek East and Latin West, the Greeks in this schema favoring themes of creation and incarnation over themes of Fall and redemption and the Latins vice versa. Anatolios goes on to demonstrate just how squarely Athanasius's understanding of creation underpins and shapes his narrative of redemption. This is a significant and substantial contribution to the volume—and indeed to Athanasian studies in general.

Fr John McGuckin offers a salutary warning against artificial systematization of the doctrine of the Fathers. Like a number of the other contributors to this volume, McGuckin is not entirely sanguine as to the possibility of Florovsky's "systematic" and "positive reconstruction of the original patristic doctrine" of the atonement. Be that as it may, McGuckin's *Preludium* presents an incisive account of the meta-history of patristic studies, cautioning against reliance on the overly-neat abstracts of patristic theology found in many modern patrologies and textbooks and arguing instead for a greater engagement with what particular Fathers actually said in their own contexts. McGuckin goes on to provide a magnificent example of such an engagement in his paper on the "Theology of Salvation in St Gregory the Theologian." Among the many riches of this paper is its reinterpretation of ransom theory and its reminder that Gregory's famous Christological dictum, "What is not assumed is not saved," derives from Origen's *Dialogue with Heraclides*. McGuckin also emphasizes the extent to which the Cross is, for Gregory, a point of entry into a doxological and profoundly Pauline account of the whole divine economy of salvation.

Alexis Torrance's paper on "Atonement in the Ascetic Fathers" provides a useful shift of emphasis onto the ways in which the individual believer might enter into and, as it were, "appropriate" Christ's universal atonement. Drawing on the Desert Fathers, St Mark the Monk, Abba Isaiah, and other monastic teachers, Torrance lucidly demonstrates the extent to which participation in the Cross and sufferings of Christ is a sine qua non of all Orthodox ascetic endeavor.

The last paper in this volume is by no means the least. In his "*In Ligno Crucis*: Atonement in the Theology of Father Georges Florovsky," Matthew Baker argues passionately and persuasively for the universality of Florovsky's approach in its deliberate encompassing of both Greek and Latin liturgical and theological traditions. While certainly wary of Anselmian and post-Anselmian notions of atonement, Florovsky was committed to constructive interaction and dialogue with the West—and a positive embrace of the West wherever possible. Baker devotes much of his attention to what he understands as the single largest issue that preoccupied Florovsky—the nature of history. It was a truly historical sense that Florovsky found lacking in Bulgakov's sophiological synthesis. The incarnation is the historical event par excellence. Redemption is to be understood as taking place in time, in history, and having "permanent continuing power throughout all history." Florovsky also detected an ahistoricism in Metropolitan Anthony Khrapovitsky's *The Dogma of Redemption* (1917), criticizing this work as having overlooked the death of Christ in its subjective and crypto-Kantian preoccupation with the sufferings of Christ. This ahistorical Christianity is, for Florovsky, no more than mere moralism. Baker draws on his impressive knowledge of edited and unedited sources to articulate a critical and constructive account of Florovsky's own understanding of the atonement. Perhaps the most intriguing insight here is the extent to which Florovsky's views appear to have evolved to give greater credence to the substitutionary nature of Christ's atonement, to such a degree that he can approve Cranmer's description of the Cross as "a full, perfect, and sufficient sacrifice, oblation, and satisfaction." This fine exploration of Florovsky's own work on the atonement serves as a fitting conclusion to this collection.

It would be false to suggest that the papers presented here may be condensed into a kind of synthesis. Like the patristic witness, these are very different voices, with differing emphases and insights. But this plurivocity is a richness furnishing eloquent testimony to the ongoing force and urgency of Florovsky's mooted retrieval of the Fathers. The theology of the Fathers is indeed an "inexhaustible storehouse." These papers have delved into that storehouse with splendid results. They have also intimated that there is plenty more to be drawn from that rich treasury.

Postscript

I have deliberately left untouched the words I wrote about Fr Matthew Baker's paper long before his untimely death (and indeed long before his ordination). As a matter of fact, we were corresponding about my revision of this introduction only a few days before his passing. I should like now, however, to underline the fittingness of the dedication of this volume to his memory. Fr Matthew Baker had a stupendous knowledge of Florovsky's work and thought-world and an almost unrivalled commitment to the perpetuation of his legacy. Some have spoken of him as a 'new' or 'second' Florovsky although I prefer to think of him as the first Matthew Baker—a theologian who was beginning to finding a distinctive voice grounded in Florovsky, certainly, but also very much his own. It is a cause of great regret to me, as to so many, that that distinctive voice was cut off before it had the opportunity to develop in all its richness and fullness. One of things he and I found particular common ground in was a shared sense of Florovsky's love for and appreciation of the Latin liturgical and theological tradition, just one example of which being the Latin tags around which Florovsky structured the treatise on the atonement presented in this volume and to which Fr Matthew's paper draws attention. I recall Matthew being delighted by my being the first (by his account) to acclaim him in Latin '*dignus es!*' shortly before his ordination (the Greek '*axios!*' being the more common form). Bearing all this in mind, it seems right and proper to close with this supplication: *Requiem aeternam dona ei, Domine, et lux perpetua luceat ei.*

Marcus Plested
Marquette University
Pentecost 2015

✠

A Sacrifice for Life:
Atonement in the Orthodox Liturgical Tradition
Irenei Steenberg

"ATONEMENT" IS A HEAVY-LADEN WORD in contemporary theological usage, a bone of contention between differing religious groups, and a term prone to definition and radical re-definition across history. The attempt to understand what "atonement" might mean in a broad patristic context, as with the focus of this symposium, is critical; but it cannot and must not be carried out apart from the liturgical framework within which the majority of Church Fathers lived and wrote. The present paper seeks to examine the testimony of Orthodox liturgical experience to a concept of "atonement"—chiefly in the Divine Liturgy and Orthodox liturgical "pre-history" in Israelite worship surrounding the Day of Atonement (*Yom Kippur*)—revealing the manner in which it is perceived as a deeply incarnational reality rooted in eucharistic participation in the divine-human person of the Son.

The Contours of "Atonement" in Liturgical Life

The shape and reality of Orthodox belief comes from the Divine Liturgy. Or rather, it comes from the whole liturgical consciousness of a Church that has, from its earliest history—and indeed, its older "prehistory"—been shaped and molded by its life of ordered worship of God. It was in the context of the ritually remembered and liturgically enacted eschatological hope of Old Testament worship that the apostles came to perceive in Jesus of Nazareth the Messiah to whom worship and prophecy, Scripture and expectation had long pointed. It was within the context of the sacrificial system of the Temple that Christ's embrace of the Cross and His unparalleled resurrection were understood by those first disciples as events that perfected a centuries-old relationship between man's sin and God's redemptive love. It was in the context of eucharistic, liturgical worship that sense could be made of the martyrs' sacrifice during the first persecutions; that apostles and fathers could discover and articulate the theological realities of suffering and redemption. And it was, perhaps above all, within the liturgical context of Orthodox life that the great theological conflicts of pivotal centuries in church history could be responded to, not as abstract philosophical or metaphysical discussions, but concrete arenas in which a lived and experienced theology might be articulated and defended in intellectual terms—in which, as the popular Latin saying goes, the *lex orandi* might be effectively spelled out as the *lex credendi*.

Taking the Divine Liturgy as the heart of this whole liturgical reality of Orthodox worship, it is important—though not at all surprising—to note that it is shot through from beginning to end with images and contexts of sacrifice, and even what we might call "atoning sacrifice" (though what we mean by this latter phrase is at the heart of our interest in this study, and a question to which we shall return). Drawn out of a sacrificial history and shaped around the self-offering of the sacrificial Christ, the Liturgy perhaps naturally has the shape of a sacrificial reality. Yet it is revealing to note the unique way in which sacrifice itself is re-presented (that is, made newly present, newly experienced) in the liturgical actions themselves. Just what is the "sacrifice" and the "atonement" that is proclaimed and lived in the Orthodox Divine Liturgy and in broader Orthodox liturgical life?

Perhaps we might begin by identifying the contours of just what is *not* proclaimed, of certain elements or visions of sacrifice and atonement that are notably absent in the Orthodox liturgical context. Taking for the moment the dominant two modern views of atonement in Christian religious contexts, namely the various forms of a ransom theory, on the one hand, and of a satisfaction theory, on the other, certain absences in the Divine Liturgy are noteworthy.[1] There is, for example, no textual language, visual imagery, or enacted motion in the Liturgy that speaks in terms of Christ's sacrifice effecting the payment of a "debt" for sin, whether to God or to the devil; there is no trace whatever in the Liturgy of Christ's sacrifice as standing in substitution for a penalty owed by man; and there is no sense in which the liturgical sacrifice is portrayed as appeasing the wrath that God might hold toward man or his sin. Let us be clear: these individual concepts are all present—there is certainly liturgical language that speaks of sin as debt, that talks of man being ransomed from death by Christ,[2] that identifies divine

---

[1]We will leave to one side for the moment the "moral influence view" of such thinkers as Paul Tillich.

[2]E.g. the prayer after "Holy, Holy, Holy" in the anaphora of St Basil the Great: "Having cleansed us by water and sanctified us with the Holy Spirit, He gave Himself as a ransom to death in which we were held captive, sold under sin"; Jacob Goar, ed., Εὐχολόγιον sive Rituale graecorum, (2d ed.; Venice: Typographia Bartholomaei Javarina, 1730), 142.

wrath[3]—but, and this is the critical point, *these are not directly connected to the liturgical emphasis on sacrifice proper.* They are identified as part of the complex reality of humanity's fluid and changing interactions with God whose nature is eternal and immutable, and the way God's consistent nature is experienced by the human race in light of the creative self-mutilation of its sin. But when Orthodox liturgical worship focuses on the atoning sacrifice offered by Christ upon the Cross—mystically experienced upon the Holy Table—its emphasis is elsewhere. Atonement itself means something different.

What, then, is its liturgical meaning? In the context of this paper, I will suggest that the Orthodox vision of "atonement", as defined by liturgical experience, is chiefly an incarnational, eucharistic concept, stressing the forging of communion between the divine and human, God and man, through participation in the incarnational unity of the Father's Son. But to arrive at this definition (which may seem rather robust, perhaps, for a term—καταλλαγή in Greek; the Russian equivalent is примирение—that appears only once in the New Testament, at Rom 5:11[4]), we must resist the urge to start anywhere other than the prayer of the Church. Our definition must come from the testimony of liturgical experience and history, and in fact in the "prehistory" of the Orthodox Liturgy: namely, the sacrificial system of the Old Testament and the Scriptures that ground it, for it is these realities that create the whole context of sacrificial theology in which Orthodox worship is rooted.

Drawn from the Old Testament: Revealing Divine Reality

It is necessary as a first step in this project to say something about the broad Orthodox vision of liturgical worship itself, which is inherited directly from a long Israelite history of worship and prayer. Namely, and as a kind of "first principle," Orthodox as well as Old Testament liturgical life is rooted in the belief that worship is something divine, revealed by God rather than fashioned by man, and revealed precisely so that there may be a created experience in the temporal world of the eternal heavenly worship that surrounds the throne of God. Earthly worship mirrors heavenly reality. In this, its source in the divine is critical, for liturgical worship is understood as an essential part of God's

---

[3]E.g. the repeated petitions in various litanies, "for our deliverance from all affliction, wrath, danger and constraint" (Goar, *Εὐχολόγιον*, 52). In the threefold litany in the Divine Liturgy of St Basil, the second petition connects wrath with "God's just rebuke," from which deliverance is begged.

[4]In most English translations (e.g. NASB, NKJV, ESV, ASV), the word in this passage is rendered as "reconciliation."

self-revelation. It is not the form that man has given to express his theology: it is the form that God has given to ground man's theology. Thus, the Lord is quite explicit in the Scriptures that the worship engaged in by His people is not to be fashioned of their design nor like that of other tribes, stating clearly that "You shall not worship the LORD your God with such things." (Deut 12:4) but in the way He has revealed. This is not left as a vague concept: precise details of liturgical actions, structures, adornments, vestments and rites are spelled out by God down to their minutiae (cf. Exod 12, 13, 25–31), even with respect to the physical places of worship ("Be careful not to sacrifice your burnt offerings anywhere you please; offer them only at the place the Lord will choose . . . and there observe everything I command you" Deut 12:13–14). This precision and exactitude are grounded in the driving understanding that it is God who has chosen and fashioned the means of right worship (cf. Deut 12:11), and that the human race is to receive it as the means of experiencing heavenly reality in the created, earthly realm.

This is an essential point, because it provides us with the framework in which to understand how it is the liturgical, worshipping reality itself that must provide the Church and her teachers with the contours for theological understanding, and not the other way around. Such liturgical worship is not perceived—either in ancient Israel or the New Israel of the Church—as an expression of right theological belief, but as the divinely revealed reality of which authentic theological writing is a compelling expression. Only when theological reflection is approached in this way—*from* divine worship *through* dogmas and theological discourses—do we preserve an authentically Orthodox approach to the very idea of speaking theological truth.

At the heart of this divine revelation that is the liturgical worship of the chosen people, we find sacrifice. From the first covenants with the patriarchs through to the full establishment of temple ritual, sacrifice stands at the heart of the worshipping life God has shown to man (and we must remember that the framework of the physical contours of the Orthodox Divine Liturgy have their origins in the temple theology of ancient Israel, shaped largely around the later structure of synagogue ritual). And if we go further still, at the heart of this whole sacrificial system stands one feast, one day, that gives meaning and measure to all others: the Day of Atonement (*Yom Kippur*). What is revealed of sacrifice and atonement in this important feast is critical in coming to understand what atonement means in Orthodox liturgical life.

The Day of Atonement: Yom Kippur

Referred to in Lev. 16:31 as "the Sabbath of Sabbaths" (σάββατα σαββάτων in the LXX; שבת שבתון in the Hebrew), the Day of Atonement is in some sense the feast around which the whole liturgical theology of worship in ancient Israel orbits. "For on that day the priest shall make atonement for you," we find written in Lev 16:30, "to cleanse you, that you may be clean from all your sins before the Lord". This cleansing (καθαρίσαι) is made a present reality on the feast through a two-fold ritual: (1) the cleansing and purification of the sanctuary, priests, and the people (cf. Lev 16:16–19, 30, 33–34); and (2) the expulsion of the sins of Israel through the casting out of the scapegoat (cf. Lev 16:10, 20–22). The first major dimension of the ritual—the cleansing and purification—is carried out through a combination of animal sacrifice preceding blood and incense offerings, through which the priest cleanses first himself (cf. Lev 16:6–14), then all the people (16:15), then the sanctuary itself and with it all the children of Israel (16:16–19, 23–25). The ritual of expelling and eradicating sin is then enacted upon the goat that has been spared the lot of the immolated offering (cf. Lev 16:8), on the head of which the priest lays his hands, confesses all the sins of the people, and sends it away into the wilderness to "bear on itself all their iniquities to an uninhabited land" (Lev 16:20–22).

Between these two facets of the Day of Atonement's liturgical structure, it is unquestionably the focus on the remission, expulsion, and eradication of sin that takes the place of greatest emphasis. While the acts of purification take place "inside the veil" (Lev 16:15)—that is, in the Holy of Holies—the immolation of the sin offering and the whole ritual of the scapegoat take place in the presence of the people as quite public spectacles. "Atonement," as that concept is given shape by this day, is an interweaving of purification and healing that leads to a renewed closeness with God, on the one hand, and the casting out of sin, on the other. But liturgically, ritually, it is emphatically on this latter theme that the day focuses most dramatically.

Nonetheless, this emphasis on the eradication of sin—which, we must remember, is always the emphasis of sin offerings and most sacrificial offerings—has a distinct and somewhat unique shape within the context of the Day of Atonement. Even within ongoing Jewish worship today, stripped as it is of the sacrificial rituals of old Israelite liturgical life, it remains a distinctive feast with a distinctive character. As described by the Modern Orthodox rabbi Dr. Irving Greenberg, Yom Kippur goes beyond the elimination of sin to the renewal of the individual. Habit and conditioning often combine with the structure of individual life to keep the person torn between evil and ethic, between apathy and ideal, between inertia and desire for improvement. Against these powerful forces which proclaim that humans cannot change, Yom Kippur teaches that there is capacity for renewal and unification of life.[5]

It is precisely this vision of "renewal and unification of life" that is of interest to us, for in this emphasis "the Sabbath of Sabbaths" reveals something essential to the whole nature of sacrificial worship, and defines "atonement" itself as something that cleanses, renews, and unifies.

The Vision of Sacrifice and Atonement in the Divine Liturgy

We are now, I believe, in a position to look at the Divine Liturgy proper, to discover what it has to say about the Orthodox understanding of atonement and Christ's atoning sacrifice for humankind.

On a basic level, we see in the Liturgy a fairly consistent mirroring of the sacrificial nature of the tabernacle and temple worship, precisely as we would suspect—with the blood sacrifices of the Old Covenant replaced by the bloodless sacrifice of the New. This is given shape within a liturgical structure that is largely molded around the edifice of post-Babylonian-Captivity synagogue worship, into which the sacrificial eucharistic themes have been inserted, as the notions of limited physical sacrifices (which separated temple ritual from the synagogues) were replaced by the Christian vision of the perfected, universal sacrifice of Christ that is made mystically present in every Liturgy.

The key ingredients of "atonement," as we found them defined by the liturgical acts of the ancient Day of Atonement, are likewise present. Within the Divine Liturgy are located quite clearly the two key themes of that day: the expulsion of the people's sin (together with that of the priests, and the purification of the temple space), as well as the preparation of human persons for union with God. However, while on the Day of Atonement we found the stronger emphasis upon the eradication and expulsion of sin, with a more secluded yet important focus on purification and unification with God, in the Divine Liturgy we find the emphasis on these dual themes dramatically reversed. In the Orthodox liturgical embrace of atonement, it is the eradication of sin that becomes the more secluded, peremptory dimension of the bloodless sacrifice,

[5]Irving Greenberg, *The Jewish Way: Living the Holidays* (New York: Touchstone, 1988), 211.

while the renewal of communion and union with God becomes the focal center-point of the whole liturgical mystery.

The Preparation of the Lamb: the Sacrificial Lamb and Sin Offering

Perhaps this observation is most significantly summed up in the fact that the chief liturgical commemoration of the sacrificial acts, tied into Christ's representation of the immolated lamb of the sin offering, is contained in the actions of the *proskomedia* (preparation of the Eucharistic elements), which takes place before the "public" Liturgy begins. We might remember that on the Day of Atonement, a portion of the festal ritual took place "behind the veil", out of the view of the people, and there the priest made unifying purification around the altar of the Lord; and that the "public" rite that took place in the presence of all the people was the immolation of the offered animal as well as the whole ritual of the scapegoat. In the Divine Liturgy there is similarly a ritual "behind the veil" (now the iconostasis), namely the *proskomedia*; as well as that which takes place in interaction with all the faithful, namely the whole service following "Blessed is the Kingdom . . ." But the focus of these two segments is here precisely the opposite: the "public liturgy" focuses on communion and union, while the focus on the physical sacrifice of the Lamb takes place at the table of oblation, behind the closed iconostasis and before the opening blessing.

How is the immolated sacrifice of the Lamb commemorated in the *proskomedia*? In the first case, each of the five incisions by which the liturgical Lamb—the center of the chief *prosphoron* (loaf offered for use as Eucharist host)—is prepared is made with a triangular liturgical implement designated a "spear," accompanied by scriptural refrains on the slaughter of the sacrificial lamb and the self-offering of the Messiah: (1) "He was led as a lamb to the slaughter" (Isa 53:7); (2) "as a sheep before its shearers is silent, So He opened not His mouth" (ibid.); (3) "In His humiliation His justice was taken away" (Acts 8:33); (iv) "Who shall declare His generation?" (ibid.); and (v) "For His life is taken from the earth" (ibid.). Then, as the inverted Lamb is cut cross-wise with the spear, the priest proclaims: "Sacrificed is the Lamb of God, that taketh away the sin of the world, for the life of the world and for its salvation" (cf. John 1:29).[6] Here we have a clear liturgical re-presentation of Christ's perfected blood-offering, in which are symbolized and commemorated simultaneously the Messianic prophecies rooted in ancient patterns of animal sacrifice, together with the events of Christ's passion leading to the Cross at Golgotha. This whole

---

[6]Goar, Εὐχολόγιον, 49.

action of preparing the Lamb is referred to by St Nicholas Cabasilas (1322/23–ca. 1391), one of the greatest Byzantine commentators on the Liturgy, as the "sacrifice of the loaf,"[7] in which

> the priest expresses in words or represents by his gestures all that he knows of the solemn sacrifice, as far as he can with the means at his disposal. Thus he shows how the Lord began His Passion, how He died, how His side was pierced with a lance, and how, as the Gospel tells us, blood and water flowed from the wound.[8]

In this last comment, Cabasilas refers to the action of the priest in piercing the side of the prepared Lamb with the liturgical spear before mingling wine and water in the chalice, quoting St John the Theologian: "one of the soldiers pierced His side with a spear, and immediately blood and water came out." (John 19:34).[9]

In this ritual of oblation, of offering and preparing the Lamb, the priest "performs ceremonies which symbolize the Cross and death of Christ,"[10] and these in fact constitute a remarkable liturgical making-present of the events of the Lord's passion. The imagery, words, and actions combine the ancient rite of the sacrificial sin offering with the Christological perfection of that ancient practice. Hence the altar of the sacrifice is the earth itself, symbolized in the paten and *asteriskos* ("star-cover") that represent the caves both of Bethlehem and Jerusalem; hence all the motions of the sacrifice are cruciform and enacted with the sign of the Cross; hence the language of the prophets is mingled with the testimony of the Gospel, and so on. This rite of Christ as sin offering culminates with the prayer of the priest over the prepared and covered gifts:

> O God, our God, Who didst send forth the Heavenly Bread, the food of the whole world, our Lord and God, Jesus Christ, the Saviour and Redeemer and Benefactor Who blesseth and sanctifieth us: Do Thou Thyself bless this offering, and accept it upon Thy most heavenly altar. As Thou art good and the lover of mankind, remember those that offer it and those for whose sake it was offered; and preserve us uncondemned in the ministry of Thy Divine Mysteries. For hallowed and glorified is Thy most honourable and majestic

---

[7]Nicholas Cabasilas, *Commentary on the Divine Liturgy*, 6.2 in SC 4 (ed. Sévérien Salaville; 1967), 80; J. M. Hussey and P. A. McNulty, trans., *Commentary on the Divine Liturgy* (London: SPCK, 1960, 1983), 34. St Nicholas is commemorated in the Orthodox calendar on June 20th.

[8]Ibid., 6.5 (SC 4bis, 82); Hussey and McNulty, 35 (translation slightly altered).

[9]Goar, Εὐχολόγιον, 50.

[10]Cabasilas, *Commentary* 8.1 (SC 4, 86); Hussey and McNulty, 36.

Name, of the Father, and of the Son, and of the Holy Spirit, now and ever, and unto the ages of ages. Amen.[11]

We might note, further, the striking way in which this liturgical service mirrors the movements prescribed in Leviticus for the Day of Atonement, wherein the sacrificial lamb is brought into the tabernacle, sacrificed there, and incensed (cf. Lev 16:6–14); which actions all take place, in the same order, in the service of the *proskomedia*.[12]

What is far more significant, however, is the very fact that it is the *proskomedia* that constitutes the chief liturgical action commemorating in a dedicated way the dimension of older Israelite worship focused on the immolated offering of sacrifice to eradicate sin. It is in this quiet ceremony of preparation, performed behind the iconostasis before the majority of the faithful have yet arrived in the temple, that the Orthodox Liturgy most profoundly emphasizes the passion and death of the Lamb offered for the eradication of human transgression.

Beyond the Proskomedia: *Inverting the Emphasis of the Older Sacrificial Vision of Atonement*

That which takes place beyond the *proskomedia*, once the Lamb has been prepared and covered, is a liturgical service in which the emphasis is rather different. Rather than focusing on the act of immolation by which the once-and-for-all perfection of the sin offering is made universal by Christ, the emphasis of the Liturgy "proper" is upon the manner in which this invokes the cleansing and purification of the people, enabling in them a new union and communion in God. From this point forward, the "atoning sacrifice" into which the people are drawn through the liturgical mystery is that of Christ's sanctification of creation and restoration of union with man and Himself. It is taken as a given throughout the Divine Liturgy that this atonement is made possible through a remission of sin, and that without such remission no union with God is possible; but henceforth the acts and the fact of sin's defeat are not what is emphasized in the liturgical participation in Christ's sacrifice. They are its preamble. The atonement experienced in the Divine Liturgy—which is "the Sacrifice of Sacrifices," just as the Day of Atonement was "the Sabbath

---

[11]Goar, Εὐχολόγιον, 51.

[12]I am not suggesting that it is possible to identify any direct link between the rubrics of the Divine Liturgy as a whole, or the *proskomedia* proper, and the structure of the rituals in Leviticus for Yom Kippur. Rather, it seems evident that much of the distinctive shape of the movement between the place before and behind the iconostasis represents an ancient tradition of practice going back to the earliest days of Israelite worship in the Tabernacle.

of Sabbaths"—is a sacrifice of union. What reemerges throughout the Liturgy
is the call for the remission of sin to be made real and present in the gathered
faithful, that the sanctifying grace of communion might be available for their
participation.

MOVEMENT TOWARD THE *ANAPHORA*

The liturgical motions that lead up to the *anaphora* and full consecration of the
Holy Gifts emphasize, in an increasingly pointed way, the manner in which the
redemption of sin opens the way for the heart of Christ's sacrificial offering: the
renewal of communion with Himself. We therefore see a transition from the
emphasis of the *proskomedia* to that of the *anaphora*, in which the groundwork
of the forgiveness of sin provides the route into the bodily and spiritual participation in the incarnate Son.

At the singing of the *Trisagion* hymn, for example, which is the "thrice-holy"
song of the angels at the throne of God, the priest prays for the people:

> Master, accept also from the mouths of us sinners this thrice-holy hymn,
> and watch over us in Thy goodness. Forgive us every transgression, voluntary
> and involuntary; sanctify our souls and bodies, and enable us to serve Thee
> in holiness all the days of our life . . .[13]

This prayer is uttered, Cabasilas says, "that the bodies and souls [of the faithful]
may be cleansed, and their sins forgiven, and that they may worship Him in
holiness all the days of their life."[14] The forgiveness of sins is a part, and a significant part, of what is nonetheless a movement towards something far greater
than merely forgiveness.

We see this again at the first Litany of the Faithful, following the reading of
the Gospel and prior to the Great Entrance. Here the priest prays mystically:

> We thank Thee, O Lord God of hosts, who hast accounted us worthy to
> stand even now before Thy Holy Altar, and to fall down before Thy com-
> passion for our sins and for the errors of all the people. Make us worthy to
> offer Thee intercessions, supplications, and bloodless sacrifices on behalf of
> all Thy people.[15]

And a few moments later, at the mystical prayer of the second Litany of the
Faithful:

[13]Goar, Εὐχολόγιον, 55.
[14]Cabasilas, *Commentary*, 21.1 (SC 4, 150); Hussey and McNulty, 60.
[15]Goar, Εὐχολόγιον, 57.

Again and at all times we fall down before Thee, O God who lovest mankind, that looking down on our petition Thou wouldst cleanse our souls and bodies from all defilement of flesh and spirit; and grant us to stand blameless and without condemnation before Thy Holy Altar. Grant also to those who pray with us, O God, growth in life and faith and spiritual understanding. Grant them always to worship Thee blamelessly with fear and love, and to partake without condemnation of Thy holy mysteries, and to be accounted worthy of Thy heavenly Kingdom . . .[16]

Again we see the escalating transition of emphasis from the necessary start-ing point of the remission of sin to the heart of what atonement and sacrifice really mean in the Orthodox liturgical context: the participation of the faithful in the unifying mystery of the Son's joining together of man and God. This is emphasized in a famous line found in the priest's long prayer before the Great Entrance, during which the prepared gifts are brought into the altar and set upon the Holy Table for what Cabasilas calls the sacrifice itself—that is, the *anaphora*. As the altar and people are censed by the deacon, the priest mysti-cally prays:

I entreat Thee, who alone art good and ready to hear: look down on me, a sinner and Thine unprofitable servant, and cleanse my soul and my heart from an evil conscience; and by the power of the Holy Spirit enable me, who am endowed with the grace of the priesthood, to stand before this, Thy Holy Altar, and perform the sacred mystery of Thy holy and pure Body and pre-cious Blood. For I draw near to Thee, and bowing my neck I implore Thee: do not turn Thy face away from me, nor cast me out from among Thy children; but account me, Thy sinful and unworthy servant, worthy to offer gifts to Thee. *For Thou art the Offerer and the Offered, the Receiver and the Received, O Christ our God*, and to Thee do we ascribe glory . . .[17]

This remarkable prayer sets the sacrifice about to be offered—the very atoning sacrifice of the Liturgy itself—into the incarnational context of Christ's uniting in Himself God and man, Creator and creature. The one who is offered is the one who makes the offering; the one who is received on the Holy Table is the one who receives; that is, the sacrifice about to be effected mystically is one in which Christ's incarnation draws together those who make the sacrifice and

---

[16]Ibid., 57–58.
[17]Ibid., 58.

Him to whom the sacrifice is made. Purified of sin, the faithful who partake of Christ's atoning sacrifice participate in Christ God Himself.[18]

THE *ANAPHORA*: THE INCARNATIONAL SACRIFICE

That which St. Nicholas Cabasilas refers to as the sacrifice proper, namely the *anaphora*, fully exemplifies the unifying vision of atonement proclaimed by and experienced in the Orthodox Divine Liturgy. As he writes, "the essential act in the celebration of the holy mysteries is the transformation of the elements into the Divine Body and Blood; its aim is the sanctification of the faithful, who through these mysteries receive the remission of their sins and the inheritance of the Kingdom of heaven."[19] That which is made possible through the forgiveness of sins is the participation in the unifying reality of the incarnation, and so the faithful, purified by prayer, draw near to the Body and Blood of Christ and receive from them a new participation in the divine life.

The telling movement of the Divine Liturgy at the *anaphora* proper reveals this fundamentally incarnational focus. Grounding the liturgical sacrifice in the foundation of the Creed and the common faith of the Church (which the Creed itself frames in Trinitarian terms, but with its focal emphasis on the mystery of the incarnation of the Son), the people respond to the deacon's charge to "offer the holy oblation in peace" with their unique reply: "a mercy of peace, a sacrifice of praise."[20] That which is to be offered in peace and mercy is the praise of the Son's incarnation, which praise draws the people into the reality itself. The movements of the anaphora then become increasingly focused on two chief facets of the economy of salvation in which the union between man and God is paramount: the participation of the apostles in the incarnate union through receiving the Body and Blood of Jesus Christ, and the transfiguring power of the Holy Spirit to effect union with Christ, exemplified in the Pentecost.

The communion of the holy apostles in Christ is obviously the chief image and the central focus of the *anaphora* prayers. In the *anaphora* of St John Chrysostom, the priest's prayer before the "words of institution" (i.e. "This is

[18]Cf. also the prayer of the priest before the Creed: "Lord God almighty, Who alone art holy, Thou acceptest the sacrifice of praise from those who call upon Thee with their whole heart. Accept also the prayer of us sinners, and lead us to Thy Holy Altar. Enable us to offer Thee gifts and spiritual sacrifices for our sins and for the errors of the people. Account us worthy to find grace in Thy sight, that our sacrifice may be acceptable to Thee, and that the good Spirit of Thy grace may dwell upon us and upon these gifts here offered, and upon all Thy people . . . ." (Ibid., 59).

[19]Cabasilas, *Commentary* 1.1 (SC 4, 56); Hussey and McNulty, 25 (translation slightly modified).

[20]Goar, Εὐχολόγιον, 60.

my Body . . . ," etc.) stresses the focus of this moment as the apostles' participation in the offering that Christ made when He "gave Himself up for the life of the world"—an offering clearly referring to the passion on the Cross, yet which the prayer frames as the concluding dimension of the "doing of all things . . . to bring us to heaven."[21] It is the Father's offering of the Son, "that whoever believes in Him should not perish but have eternal life,"[22] that is the full mystery in which the apostles commune at the mystical supper.

This is yet clearer in the *anaphora* of St Basil the Great. In the equivalent prayer there, we find the "words of institution" prefaced by a much longer prayer recounting the economy of salvation, in which the mystery about to participated in is described as that of the Saviour being

> born of a woman, the holy Theotokos and ever virgin Mary; born under the law, to condemn sin in His flesh, so that those who died in Adam may be brought to life in Him, Thy Christ.[23]

As at the Liturgy of St John, that offering "for life"[24] in which the apostles partake through Christ's sanctification of the bread and wine is the whole mystery of the Son's incarnation. This incarnation is, in the Divine Liturgy, seen in cosmic terms: both *anaphoras* begin the account that culminates in the Eucharist, with references to creation (St John's proclaiming, "Thou it was who brought us from non-existence into being", while St Basil's refers to God "having made man by taking dust from the earth and honouring him with Thine image . . .")[25]; and both lead beyond the mystical supper to the eschaton (before the elevation of the gifts, the priest at St John's *anaphora* calls to mind "the Cross, the tomb, the resurrection on the third day, the ascension into heaven, the sitting on the right hand and the second and glorious coming again"; while in St Basil's *anaphora* the priest commemorates "His saving passion and life-giving Cross, His three-day burial and resurrection from the dead, His ascension into heaven, His enthronement at Thy right hand, O God and Father, and His glorious and awesome second coming"[26]). The participation in the Body and Blood thus stand mystically at the center of cosmic history, the Alpha and the Omega present outside of time, uniting beginnings and ends, creatures and

[21]From the prayer before "Holy, Holy, Holy" (Goar, *Εὐχολόγιον*, 61).
[22]John 3:16, quoted in the anaphora prayer, after the "Holy, Holy, Holy" (ibid., 61).
[23]Ibid., 142.
[24]St Basil's anaphora includes a phrase reminiscent of St John's, referring to "the night . . . on which He was delivered up for the life of the world" (ibid., 143).
[25]Ibid., 60–61 and 142.
[26]Ibid., 62 and 143.

their Creator, temporal man and the eternal, infinite God. Communion in the "cosmic Christ"[27] is thus the fruit of the eucharistic sacrifice—not a participation in one or another act (even so great an act as that of ascending the Cross), but the whole reality of Him who "took flesh",[28] who is the "Lamb slain from the foundation of the world".[29]

Together with this participation in the incarnate Christ through the Body and Blood, the Liturgy emphasizes also the role of the Holy Spirit in effecting the union between God and man by which the atonement of sin is accomplished. In the *anaphora* of St Basil, the priest immediately follows the threefold "amen" of the *epiclesis* (invocation of the Holy Spirit) with the petition, "unite us all to one another who become partakers of the one Bread and Cup in the communion of the one Spirit," whereas the *anaphora* of St John's explicitly refers to the transformation of the gifts by the power of the Spirit ("... changing them by Thy Holy Spirit: Amen, amen, amen"). The Russian Orthodox practice of inserting the prayer of the Third Hour[30] as a priestly devotional within the *epiclesis* further stresses the manner in which the nature of God as Trinity is experienced liturgically through the deliberate interweaving of the Father's offering of the Son with the transformative power of the Spirit. It also ties together the historical experiences of the Mystical Supper and the Pentecost, seeing the sacrifice of Christ in terms not simply of the Cross and death, but of the whole incarnational mystery that includes the sending of the Paraclete and the transformation of the disciples' hearts.

[27]A phrase that has become rather popular in contemporary scholarship, and which has the potential to be quite helpful, so long as it is not used in the manner exemplified in Teilhard de Chardin's embrace of a "Christ consciousness" (such as in his *Christianity and Evolution*) or Matthew Fox's rather bizarre mysticism, in *The Coming of the Cosmic Christ: The Healing of Mother Earth and the Birth of a Global Renaissance* (Harper & Row, 1988), but rather to emphasize that the incarnate Christ is not merely an historical figure, but the eternal Son of the Father and the Creator, a person in whom all history is contained and who is the foundation of history itself. Florovsky himself had a strong sense of the cosmic dimensions of sin (calling it a "cosmic catastrophe"), of the created order in God's design (a "cosmic harmony"), and of the salvation of man united to Christ (a "cosmic transfiguration"); see "Redemption," 105–106 and 115.

[28]John 1:14.

[29]Rev 13:8; cf. 1 Pet 1:18–20, 1 Cor 2:7–10. The line is quoted by Florovsky in "Redemption," 100, where he notes: "The mystery of the Cross begins in eternity, 'in the sanctuary of the Holy Trinity, unapproachable for creatures.' And the transcendent mystery of God's wisdom and love is revealed and fulfilled in history. Hence Christ is spoken of as the Lamb, 'who was foreknown indeed before the foundation of the world' (Peter [*sic*] 1:19), and even 'that hath been slain from the foundation of the world' (Rev. 13:8)."

[30]"O Lord, Who didst send down Thy most Holy Spirit upon Thine apostles at the third hour: take Him not from us, O Good One, but renew Him in us who pray unto Thee"; in *Great Books of Hours, Ὡρολόγιον τὸ Μέγα* (Athens: Apostoliki Diakonia, 1963; 16th repr. 2005), 103.

This profound liturgical movement, from creation to the eschaton and centered on the presence of the incarnate, cosmic Christ, finds its culmination in the participation in the Body and Blood by the faithful. Here the communicant finds himself actively in the experience of the atonement of his sins—for in this moment, he experiences in his person true communion with God, from whom his sin had formerly created an impassable chasm. Here he finds his sins forgiven, yes; but far more than this, he finds his life drawn up into the life of God, his heart purified and made to a new degree a temple of the Holy Spirit—his life given perfectly to the Father. Drawing all these themes together, the prayers after the consecration in the Liturgy of St John Chrysostom include the important affirmation:

> That to those who partake of them, [the Holy Gifts] may be for the vigilance of soul, for the remission of sins, for the communion of Thy Holy Spirit, for the fulfillment of the Kingdom of heaven, for boldness towards Thee, and not for judgment or condemnation.[31]

The person for whom atonement is thus made is united to his God. This is, as Fr Georges Florovsky was to put it, the "very essence of salvation." In his words:

> In that lifting up of human nature into an everlasting communion with the Divine Life, the Fathers of the early Church unanimously saw the very essence of salvation, the basis of the whole redeeming work of Christ. 'That is saved which is united with God,' says St Gregory of Nazianzus.[32]

What Conclusions Can Be Drawn on the Nature of "Atonement"?

It is my suggestion in this paper that if we use this experienced reality of the Divine Liturgy, grounded in an awareness of its prehistory in older Israelite worship, to answer the question "What is the Orthodox understanding of atonement?", we are given the contours of a clear response:

1) Atonement is chiefly the establishment of communion between man and God, which has its substance in the communion of human and divine in the incarnate Christ. It is above all an incarnational reality, not a mere fiat or alteration in external relationship. The chief act by which the Son atones for the sin of mankind—that is, for the separation and division caused by man's sin—is in "becoming flesh and dwelling among us" (John 1:14).

---

[31]Goar, Euchologion, 62
[32]"Redemption," 95–96.

2) Since atonement refers to the healing of the separation of sin and a resto-ration of man's communion in God, it necessarily involves the forgiveness of sin; and this forgiveness is made real through the ancient means of sacrifice. Yet the sacrifice here is not of appeasement but of self-offering: it is the Son's offering Himself into life and death that brings His forgiving love into every dimension of sinful human experience, restoring it thereby. Without this sacrificial offer-ing for the forgiveness of sins, the atonement of sin—that is, the healing of its divisions and bringing of man back into divine communion—cannot take place; yet the atonement of sin is not to be confused (as is so often the case) with the act of forgiveness itself.

3) In this light, the once-for-all offering of Christ upon the Cross—the perfection and conclusion of blood offerings—cannot be seen as the key "ingre-dient" of what atonement means, except inasmuch as it is viewed as an integral part of the incarnational self-sacrifice of the Father's Son, perfected only in the Eucharistic participation in His Body and Blood.[33] A statement such as "Christ atoned for our sins upon the Cross" is incomplete, from the testimony of the Church's liturgical practice, until we see the work of the Cross as completed in the chalice. The atonement for sins did not happen at a moment in the past: it happens at the moment of man's communion in the divine mystery of Christ's Body and Blood, when the joining-together of God and man that took place in Bethlehem, that reached throughout all of life and even death through the Cross, that defeated death in the Resurrection, is made real and present in the faithful communicant who receives into his human body, and is joined bodily and spiritually with, the divine-human person of the incarnate Son.

The Role of Liturgical Testimony in Shaping the Writings of the Fathers

Finally, I would like to conclude with a few remarks on the influence this litur-gical context has on the Fathers, and what influence it ought to have on our attempts to understand the concept of atonement in the patristic tradition.

It ought to go without saying—though, given the testimony of what we too often see in patristic scholarship today, it nonetheless needs to be said—that the experience of the Church's liturgical life forms the core and central context of the whole patristic tradition. The Fathers of the Church are not first and foremost theologically astute minds who fashion inspired doctrinal discussions

---

[33]So Florovsky in "Redemption," 101: "The sacrifice of Christ cannot be considered as a mere offering or surrender. That would not explain the necessity of the death. For the whole life of the Incarnate One was one continuous sacrifice."

to which the worshipping Church may turn for support and guidance. They are above all worshipping Christians shaped by liturgical experience, for whom the divine revelation of liturgical reality provides the root knowledge that is articulated and expressed in tracts, treatises, sermons, and conciliar documents. When the Fathers come to address specific theological issues such as Christology, Trinitarian articulation, etc., it is above all else liturgical experience that grounds their thoughts and words, and which provides the contours for their responses to the alternative views put forward in theological contexts.

This fact helps us to understand somewhat how the Fathers could reply so definitively to various speculative questions in Christian history. Thus, for example, St Irenaeus of Lyons was confronted with what was in many ways a rationally "sensible" and exegetically plausible theory of the innate deficiency of all material creation (i.e. the dualism behind what is today often called Gnosticism), and one for which both ancient Scriptures and current Christian traditions and writings were called upon for support. Yet St Irenaeus could respond with such conviction against these readings of Scripture precisely because they did not conform to the experienced revelation of Christian worship, in which the eucharistic participation in Christ's assumption of material human nature proclaims the goodness of the creature.

And thus it is throughout the whole heritage of the Fathers, from the earliest generations through to our own day. The Fathers of the Church are, in a consistent way, the mouthpieces for the Church's liturgical revelation of the Kingdom. It is through their pens that the universal experience of Christian worship is given expression and articulation; and it is this reality of the Fathers expressing liturgical experience that unites the patristic witness across history much more effectively than any forced concept of a *consensus patrum*, and which rather diminishes the need to create a "patristic synthesis," neo- or otherwise. The synthesis of the Fathers is the Divine Liturgy of the Church, and with it her whole liturgical life. It is here that they have their common voice, their common vision, and their common truth.

It is thus to this liturgical consciousness that we, too, must look as students of the Fathers, seeking to understand their views on "atonement," "sacrifice," or any other point of theological clarity. Without understanding how the Church's liturgical life bears witness to the nature of atoning sacrifice, we will never be able to understand how a St Irenaeus, a St Athanasius, a St Gregory, or any other Fathers come to speak in the way they do about the concept. If, however, we begin in the same place they began, in the liturgical mystery of atonement experienced, of union restored, and life transfigured, then the testimony of the

Fathers becomes newly accessible to a modern generation seeking articulation of these same ecclesiastical realities.

✠

Irenaeus on "Atonement"
John Behr

O NE OF THE DIFFICULTIES IN STUDYING a figure like St Irenaeus, the late second-century bishop of Lyons—who had known Polycarp, who in turn had known the apostle John—is simply the distance from which he speaks to us. We have become so used to the classical categories of Christian theology—Trinitarian Theology, Creation, Fall, Incarnation, Atonement, Ecclesiology, and so on—that they seem to us to be a given part of the Christian revelation itself. But they are not. The theologians of the first centuries did not work with these categories in mind: they did not think of themselves as developing a Trinitarian theology; nor did they think that once they had "done" Trinitarian theology, they could move on to Christology (following our textbooks of the history of theology, dividing the controversies of the early centuries according to the chapter headings of modern dogmatic textbooks). They did not think of "incarnation" as something separate from "atonement," or all of this as separate from liturgy, the fundamental framework of early Christian life and reflection, which yet rarely makes it into textbooks on the history of doctrine. A striking example of what happens when this distance is not recognized is the startling comment of Hanson on Athanasius' work *On the Incarnation*: "One of the curious results of this theology of Incarnation is that it almost does away with a doctrine of the Atonement. Of course, Athanasius believes in the Atonement, in Christ's death as saving, but he cannot really explain why Christ should have died."[1] Yet Athanasius specifically states that his intention in this work is to demonstrate that *the one on the Cross* is the *Logos* of God, and therefore the Christian faith is not *alogos*—irrational. Athanasius is not using the word "incarnation" as we have come to use it, but he is certainly not doing away with the atonement.

If reading Athanasius is beguilingly difficult, it is even more so with Irenaeus. He stands not on the verge of a recognizable Nicene orthodoxy, but as the first voice articulating a comprehensive theological vision, the first exposition of a self-confident orthodox catholic standpoint, yet one whose feet, therefore,

[1]R. P. C. Hanson, *The Search for the Christian Doctrine of God: The Arian Controversy, 318–381* (Edinburgh: T & T Clark, 1988), 450.

stand prior to that—prior to there being a New Testament, appeal to tradition, apostolic succession, and all the elements that become the standard framework of Christianity thereafter.

It is not surprising that Gustaf Aulen, in what was to become one of the landmark works on atonement in the past century, turned to Irenaeus for his starting point, even before returning to the New Testament, for Irenaeus offers a wealth of reflections on the subject (before the "New Testament" as such), and so provides an alternative point of entry into material than what has since become customary.[2] Instead of the "satisfaction theory of atonement," the polarization of this into subjective and objective versions, and the supposition that these are the only two possibilities, Aulen attempted to rehabilitate the older, more physical theory of redemption, in which the atonement was seen in terms of a divine conflict, Christ's fight against and triumph over the evil powers of this world, primarily the devil, who holds man in bondage and suffering, or Christ's payment of a ransom to death, the devil or God, so reconciling, in Himself, the world to God.

But if we are to get back to what Irenaeus was saying (so far as we can), not only do we need to overcome the contrast between "satisfaction theories" of atonement and "physical theories" (with the implicit assertion that the latter are really rather mythological and primitive), but we might also need to overcome the contrast between incarnation and atonement that plagued Hanson, and with which Fr Georges Florovsky struggled in his profound essay on Redemption. Florovsky begins this work with the statement:

> "The Word became flesh": in this is the ultimate joy of the Christian faith. In this is the fullness of revelation ... In the Incarnation human history is completed. God's eternal will is accomplished, "the mystery from eternity hidden and to angels unknown."[3]

Yet the very next paragraph seems to indicate that there is in fact something more:

> But the climax of the Gospel is the Cross, the death of the Incarnate. Life has been revealed in full through death. This is the paradoxical mystery of the Christian faith."[4]

---

[2] Gustaf Aulen, *Christus Victor: A Historical Study of the Three Main Types of the Idea of Atonement* (trans. A. G. Herbert; London: SPCK, 1931; repr. Eugene, OR: Wipf and Stock Publishers, 2003).

[3] "Redemption," 95.

[4] Ibid., 96.

Are "incarnation" and "atonement" really two distinct moments? Are "incarnation" and "atonement" the opening and the final acts, distinct but belonging to the same movement? Or does the term "incarnation" include all aspects of the work of Christ, "the fullness of revelation" rather than simply the act of a divine person becoming human? After all, we cannot even speak of the former—the "incarnation"—until the latter—the crucifixion and exaltation—is complete, for only then do we know who He is. Yet, by that point, we no longer know Him in the flesh (2 Cor 5:16), for in fact those who take up the cross are now His body.

The elements that are held apart in our systematic exposition of theology cohere together in their genesis and always need to be thought together.[5] When we turn back to Irenaeus, we will find that we need to take one further step, which is to hold together creation *and* salvation, creation and Christ's sacrifice, creation and atonement—*together*. Not—to put it somewhat crudely—as Plan A followed, after a human hiccup, by Plan B, but rather as two aspects of the one economy of God. If we want to understand how Irenaeus views the economy of God as single, as one, we need to consider the role of death in the economy, to see in Christ's own atoning death something more than a "rescue mission." In a sense, it is all how you look at it.

The Sign of Jonah

As an example of Irenaeus's approach to this, let us take the Scriptural image used by Christ Himself to explain His own work: the sign of Jonah, treated profoundly, though briefly, by Irenaeus in *Against the Heresies* 3.20.[6] He begins by explaining that God was patient with our apostasy, both because He already foresaw the victory which would be granted to the human being through the Word, and because, following the words of Christ to Paul that His strength is made perfect in weakness (2 Cor 12:9), Irenaeus suggests that it is in this way, through our own weakness and mortality, that God reveals His goodness and magnificent power.[7]

[5]As Rowan Williams notes, "Theology, in short, is perennially tempted to be seduced by the prospect of bypassing the question of how it *learns* its own language"; *On Christian Theology* (Oxford: Blackwell, 2000), 131.

[6]Hereafter cited as *AH*. Greek edition with French translation in: *Contre les hérésies*, Books 1–3 in SC 263–264, 293–294, 210–11 (ed. and trans. Adelin Rousseau and Louis Doutreleau; 1979, 1982, 1974); Book 4 in SC 100 (ed. and trans. Rousseau, et al.; 1965); Book 5 in SC 152–3 (ed. and trans. Rousseau, Doutreleau and Charles Mercier; 1969). *AH* 3.20 (SC 211, 382–99).

[7]*AH* 3.20.1 (SC 211, 382).

As an example of this, Irenaeus gives the case of Jonah, who, by God's arrangement, was swallowed up by the whale, not that he should perish, but that, having been cast out, he might be more obedient to God, and so glorify more the One who had unexpectedly saved him. He then continues:

> ... so also, from the beginning, God did bear human beings to be swallowed up by the great whale, who was the author of transgression, not that they should perish altogether when so engulfed, but arranging in advance the finding of salvation, which was accomplished by the Word, through the "sign of Jonah" (Matt 12:39–40), for those who held the same opinion as Jonah regarding the Lord, and who confessed, and said, "I am a servant of the Lord, and I worship the Lord God of heaven, who made the sea and the dry land" (Jonah 1:9), that human beings, receiving an unhoped-for salvation from God, might rise from the dead, and glorify God, and repeat, "I cried to the Lord my God in my affliction, and he heard me from the belly of Hades" (Jonah 2:2), and that they might always continue glorifying God, and giving thanks without ceasing for that salvation which they have obtained from him, "that no flesh should glory in the Lord's presence" (1 Cor 1:29), and that human beings should never adopt an opposite opinion with regard to God, supposing that the incorruptibility which surrounds them is their own by nature, nor, by not holding the truth, should boast with empty superciliousness, as if they were by nature like to God.[8]

For Irenaeus, then, God has borne the human race, from the beginning, while it was swallowed up by the whale. There is, according to this passage, no lost golden age of primordial perfection, a time when, hypothetically (and counterfactually) we might not have needed Christ.[9]

---

[8]Ibid.; my translation, based on that in *Against the Heresies*, trans. Alexander Roberts and James Donaldson, ANF 1 (1885, 1987), 450.

[9]Irenaeus does nevertheless write of the pre-lapsarian existence of Adam in occasional comments and discussion in *Against the Heresies*, e.g. *AH* 3.22–3 (SC 211, 430–69); the comments here, however, are made within the Pauline Adam-Christ framework. In the *Demonstration*, 11–16, Irenaeus provides a sustained commentary on the creation and paradisiacal life of Adam and Eve; here, it is to be noted, the theology that Irenaeus develops out of the opening chapters of Genesis is that of the dependency of the human race on God and the need for grateful obedience, human infancy, and their need for growth. That is, it functions, within the *Demonstration*, to establish the framework within which salvation history unfolds. Extant Armenian version of the *Demonstration*: Karapet Ter Merkerttschian and S. G. Wilson, eds., *Patrologia Orientalis* 12 (1919), 653–746; for an English translation see *St Irenaeus of Lyons: On the Apostolic Preaching* (trans. John Behr; Crestwood, NY: Saint Vladimir's Seminary Press, 1997).

Such language, which one can find in other fathers, sounds strange to us, largely, I suspect, because we are so accustomed to thinking of God in rather all-too-human, temporal terms: imagining Him "before" creation, deciding what He is going to do (Plan A); and then, after we messed up this plan, having to respond with Plan B (so that Christ would be Plan B). But, as Irenaeus asserts repeatedly throughout his work, theological reflection is not to start from any other (hypothetical or counterfactual) position, conceiving another God or another Christ, other than the ones proclaimed by the apostles, in accordance with the Scriptures.[10] We are, rather, to seek out the wisdom of God made manifest in the Christ preached by the apostles, the Word, Wisdom, and Power of God.

For Irenaeus, the starting point for all theological reflection is the given fact of the work of Christ, His life-giving and saving death. In a very interesting way, this is confirmed by James Barr, when he points out that it is only from the perspective of the crucified and exalted Christ that we can speak about a "Fall" in Genesis and of the human race being held thereafter under sin and death.[11] So it is that in the previous passage, Irenaeus writes of God "arranging in advance the finding of salvation, which was accomplished by the Word through the sign of Jonah"; this is already a given, though it is unknown to human beings, whom God allows to be swallowed up so that they will receive a salvation "unhoped-for" but nevertheless divinely foreseen. Creation and salvation, for Irenaeus, are not Plan A and Plan B. Rather, they cohere together as the one economy of God, which culminates in the work of Christ, but which is only understood and told from this starting point.

According to Irenaeus, this does not mitigate the responsibility of humans for their action of apostasy, nor the reality of the work of the devil in instigating this; he is, as Irenaeus put it in the passage quoted above, "the author of transgression." The devil's temptation, according to Irenaeus, is to offer what he could not give; Adam and Eve were beguiled under "the pretext of immortality."[12] So, for Irenaeus, seen in this way, death is the result of human apostasy, turning away from the one and only source of life; it is instigated by the devil and so the expression of his dominion over the human race.

[10] *AH* 1.10.3 (SC 264, 160–66).

[11] James Barr, *The Garden of Eden and the Hope of Immortality* (Minneapolis: Fortress Press, 1993), 89: "In fact, as I have shown, large elements in the text [of Genesis] cannot be made to support Paul's use of the story without distortion of their meaning. And, as I have indicated, it is not hard to suggest an alternative and intermediate position: Paul was not interpreting the story in and for itself; he was really *interpreting Christ* through the use of images from this story."

[12] *AH* 3.23.5, 4.Pref.4 (SC 211, 456–60; SC 100, 386–90).

But death is also embraced within the divine economy, the way everything fits together in God's hand. When viewed from the perspective of the salvation granted by Christ through "the sign of Jonah," we can see that, as it was God Himself who appointed the whale to swallow up Jonah, so also the engulfing of the human race by the great whale was "borne" by God in His arrangement, His economy, which culminates in the finding of salvation accomplished by the sign of Jonah.

There is an important change of perspective involved in this, of which we need to be cognizant. This change of perspective is something that runs through the whole of Scripture. It is seen clearly in Joseph's words to his brothers: "Do not be angry with yourselves because you sold me here, for God sent me before you to preserve life" (Gen 45:5). It is seen most clearly with respect to the death of Christ in the preaching of Peter in the second chapter of Acts: This Jesus, "being delivered by the determined purpose and foreknowledge of God, you have taken[a] by lawless hands, have crucified, and put to death" (Acts 2:23). Jesus was put to death by lawless hands, and it seemed to be a catastrophe, but the same event, with further reflection, is seen to be inscribed within God's plan, His economy.

This transition is seen very clearly in the move from the Synoptics to the Gospel of John. In the Synoptics, the disciples flee in fear at the Crucifixion, denying Christ, and only finally understand who Christ is after the Passion, when the risen Christ (whom they do not initially recognize) opens the Scriptures and breaks bread; they recognize Him, but He immediately disappears from sight (Luke 24). Only now do they know that this is the one spoken of in Scripture, that He is, for instance, the suffering servant spoken of by Isaiah, the one who, although no guile was found on His lips, nevertheless willingly bore our sins upon Himself, silent as a lamb, going to the slaughter, to offer propitiation to God (Isa 53). Only by the end do they know that He went voluntarily to His death as one over whom death had no hold, for He was sinless, so giving Himself in a total and absolute self-offering, a full and pure sacrifice.

And this is the point at which the Gospel of John begins: after the prologue, the Baptist cries out, "Behold! the lamb of God" (John 1:29). Then when Philip tells Nathanael that "we have found the one of whom Moses in the law and the prophets wrote," Christ subsequently tells him, "You will see greater things than these" (John 1:44–51). Thereafter, John depicts Christ as the exalted Lord, who repeatedly tells His disciples that He is from above and they from below. And so, if Christ goes to the Cross, He does so voluntarily, so that His elevation on the Cross *is* His exaltation in glory.

This is also a transition that is emphasized rhetorically in the Anaphora of St John Chrysostom, from the words, "in the night in which he was given up," to the apparent correction, "no rather, gave himself up . . ." It is necessary to be aware of this movement—from a human, historical perspective to a divine, eternal (timeless) perspective—if we are to understand how Irenaeus approaches the saving death of Christ, for it enables a transition from seeing death as catastrophic to seeing it as embraced within the divine economy. So, Irenaeus continues in the passage we were considering:

> Such then was the patience of God, that human beings, passing through all things and acquiring knowledge of death, then attaining to the resurrection from the dead, and learning by experience from whence they have been delivered, may thus always give thanks to the Lord, having received from him the gift of incorruptibility, and may love him the more, for "he to whom more is forgiven, loves more" (cf. Luke 7:42–3), and may themselves know how mortal and weak they are, but also understand that God is so immortal and powerful as to bestow immortality on the mortal and eternity on the temporal, and that they may also know the other powers of God made manifest in themselves, and, being taught by them, may think of God in accordance with the greatness of God. For the glory of the human being is God, while the vessel of the workings of God, and of all his wisdom and power is the human being.[13]

God is thus patient, while humans learn by experience their own weakness and death in their ungrateful apostasy, knowing that, having passed through this experience and having an unhoped-for salvation bestowed upon them, they will remain ever more thankful to God, willing to accept from Him the eternal existence which He alone can give.

In this way human beings become fully acquainted with the power of God: by being reduced to nothing, to dust in the earth, human beings simultaneously come to know their total dependence upon God, allowing God to work in and through them, to deploy His power in them as the recipient of all His work. Irenaeus takes Christ's words to Paul, that His "strength is made perfect in weakness" (2 Cor 12:9) as paradigmatic for the human race. Both dimensions of this economy—the engulfing of man and the salvation wrought by the Word—are simultaneously represented by Jonah, a sign of both the transgressing human race and its Saviour.

---

[13]*AH* 3.20.2 (SC 211, 388).

So, starting from the work of Christ—His satisfying, atoning, and death-destroying death, which was divinely (but not humanly) foreseen and foreshadowed in the sign of Jonah—Irenaeus can see, in the apparent tragedy and absurdity of death, the Wisdom of God being deployed, playing an educational role within the divine economy. This Wisdom enables humans to experience to the uttermost their weakness and mortality in their apostasy from God, the only source of life, so that they might thereafter hold ever more firmly to God.

Thus, while apostasy and death are nothing less than a catastrophe—as the being created by God for communion with Him in His glory turns his back on God and rots in the earth—the Wisdom of God is so powerful that even this catastrophe can be encompassed within a larger, divine economy, and so be turned to good effect. The apostasy is the victory of the devil, against which conquered human beings were too weak to fight back and obtain the prize of victory, as Irenaeus puts it.[14] The victory could only be won by the Word of God Himself, becoming incarnate. But this victory over death is something that He accomplishes in no other way than by the act of death itself—the sign of Jonah—again turning the apparently catastrophic inside out. From different perspectives, we can therefore discern two dimensions to the apostasy and death: catastrophic and pedagogic. Yet these are only a matter of perspective; for Irenaeus, there is but the one economy of the one God, which is unfolded in Scripture.

Although written several centuries later, a hymn of St John of Damascus, now used in the funeral service, gives a very beautiful poetic expression of this paradox:

> I weep and I wail when I think upon death, and behold our beauty, fashioned after the image of God, lying in the tomb, disfigured, dishonored, bereft of form. O marvel! What is this mystery which befalls us? Why have we been given over unto corruption, and why have we been wedded to death? Of a truth, as it is written, by the command of God, who gives the departed rest.[15]

Death is a catastrophe—we should weep and wail; but, it is also a marvel, a miracle, a mystery (a "sacrament")—to which we have been wedded, by the command of God, no less.

---

[14]*AH* 3.18.2 (SC 211, 344).

[15]*Idiomelon* hymn, by St. John of Damascus, in the funeral service; also as *Sticheron* from the *Aposticha*, Friday Evening Vespers, *Octôêchos*, Mode Pl. IV, in Παρακλητικὴ ἤτοι Ὀκτώηχος ἡ Μεγάλη (Athens: Apostoliki Diakonia, 1976; 4th repr. 2000), 389.

Growth and Experience

In *AH* 4.37–39, Irenaeus provides further reasons why human beings need to experience weakness and death before being glorified by God.[16] In this passage, he is responding to those who ask why God did not make human beings perfect from the beginning, such that they would never have turned away from Him. Irenaeus's response is that only *free* creatures are capable of love; and, moreover, only free creatures, capable of initiative and response, are capable of growth, and so capable of growing from their created state into the immortality and incorruptibility of God, entering into communion with Him and so being transfigured.

Moreover, Irenaeus argues, it is only by experience of contrasts that we come to know the value of gifts. For instance, the faculty of vision is valued more by those who know what it is like to be without sight. Irenaeus explains in *AH* 4.39 that this is because these valuations are based on two types of knowledge: one gained by experience and one arrived at by opinion. As the tongue learns of bitterness and sweetness only through experience, Irenaeus claims that the mind also receives the knowledge of what is good—obedience to God, which is the true life of human beings—only through the experience of both good and evil—the evil being disobedience, which is death.

The value of this experiential knowledge is that by having experience of both and rejecting disobedience by means of repentance, human beings can become ever more tenacious in their obedience to God. But, Irenaeus suggests, if human beings ever try to avoid the knowledge of both of these, the twofold faculty of knowledge, they forget themselves and kill their humanity.[17]

So Irenaeus concludes his reflections:

> God therefore has borne all these things for our sake, in order that, having been instructed through all things, henceforth we may be scrupulous in all things and, having been taught how to love God in accordance with reason, to remain in His love: God exhibiting patience in regard to the apostasy of the human being, and the human being being taught by it, as the prophet says: "Your own apostasy shall instruct you" (Jer 2:19).[18]

Irenaeus again inscribes human apostasy into the unfolding of the divine economy, and now, in fact, as with the sign of Jonah, it becomes a salvific moment.

[16]SC 100, 918–73.
[17]*AH* 4.39.1 (SC 100, 960–65).
[18]*AH* 4.37.7 (SC 100, 942–43).

In *AH* 4.38, Irenaeus approaches the same problem from a different angle. He argues that God could have created the human race perfect or as "gods" from the beginning, for all things are possible to Him. However, created things, by virtue of being created, are of a later date than their Creator—they are infantile, and so unaccustomed to, and unexercised in, perfect conduct. As it is possible for a mother to give an infant solid food from the beginning (although it would not do the infant any good), so also God could have made human beings perfect from the beginning; but humans, still in their infancy, could not have received this perfection. As creatures, we can never be uncreated; but the aim of creation is that human beings should come to be ever more fully in the image and likeness of the uncreated God. This is a process to which there is no end: human perfection lies in their continual submission to the creative activity of God, through which they are brought to share in the glory of the Uncreated.[19]

Finally, Irenaeus concludes *AH* 4.38 by sketching the preceding discussion in a few brief strokes:

> It was necessary, first, for nature to be manifest; after which, for what was mortal to be conquered and swallowed up by immortality, and the corruptible by incorruptibility, and for the human being to be made in the image and likeness of God, having received the knowledge of good and evil.[20]

Thus, again, according to Irenaeus, God was patient in the face of the apostasy of humans. He explains this within the framework of God's overall economy, by the general principle of the need for newly created human beings to acquire experience, both of good and evil, in order to hold ever more firmly onto the good and to continue indefinitely progressing towards God, becoming ever more fully in His image and likeness.

Preexistence of the Saviour

This inscription of human apostasy within the overarching single economy of God (rather than an ad hoc "rescue mission") demonstrates the omnipotence of God: He is not forced to react (to the devil's mischief or the failings of humans), to provide, as it were, in a second act, a band-aid. Instead, by the work of God in Christ, we can now see God's creative act from a new perspective, transforming what appeared to be negative into something positive, and integrating, or sublimating, both creation and apostasy into the definitive, once-for-all work of God in Christ in His atoning work, reconciling the human being to God.

[19] *AH* 4.38.3 (SC 100, 952–57).
[20] *AH* 4.38.4 (SC 100, 960–61). Cf. 2 Cor 5:4; 1 Cor 15:53; Gen 1:26, 3:5, 3:22.

Irenaeus is able to do this precisely because, as noted earlier, he is theologizing at that primitive moment of history, still in the immediacy of the Passion, rather than after a history of controversies and conclusions for which a systematic account is needed. The completeness with which this applies to Irenaeus is shown by one of his most dramatic statements, following on from the Apostle's description of Adam as the "type of the One to come" (Rom 5:14):

> Hence, also Adam himself was termed by Paul "the type of the One who was to come," because the Word, the Maker of all things, prefigured in him the economy that was to come of the humanity in regard to the Son of God; God having established that the first human being should be psychical, namely, that he should be saved by the spiritual. For, since He who saves already existed, it was necessary that the one who would be saved should come into existence, that the One who saves should not exist in vain.[21]

In Adam the Word prefigured or sketched out in advance the fullness of the human being that would be manifested in Christ; hence, Adam is a type of the One to come. However, the One who was to come existed before Adam (as the seal does before the imprint) and so it was by Him and for Him that Adam came into being. So, although only appearing at the end, this One is indeed the Beginning.[22] Creation and salvation are not distinct for Irenaeus, but are, rather, the one economy, told from the perspective of the crucifixion and resurrection, as it is only at this point that the Lord opens the books, showing that it is all about Him.

This passage also introduces another Pauline theme: that the first Adam was psychical, while the last is spiritual, referring both to Gen 2:7, where it is said that God breathed a πνοὴ ζωῆς into his nostrils so that man became a ψυχὴ ζῶσα, and to 1 Cor 15:45, where the last Adam is described as a πνεῦμα ζωοποιοῦν. Adam was established as a psychical being, animated by the breath of life; as a type of, and to be saved by, the Spiritual One, who was vivified by the Spirit. The apostasy did not transform an originally spiritual Adam into a merely psychical being. Through the apostasy Adam and Eve lost the "strength" of the breath of life; they did not "lose" the Spirit. For Irenaeus, the Spirit was certainly present with Adam in paradise, yet never ceased being present with the human race throughout the foreseen apostasy. But the Spirit was present with Adam and the human race in a preparatory manner, typifying the fullness that was and still is to come.

---

[21]*AH* 3.22.3 (SC 211, 438–39).
[22]Cf. *AH* 1.10.3 (SC 264, 160–67); *AH* 4.34.4 (SC 100, 854–61).

Irenaeus understands creation and salvation, *together*, as God's activity fashioning His handiwork, the human being, bringing humans, when they allow themselves to be skillfully fashioned, to the stature of the Saviour. The starting point for this economy is the Saviour Himself, and so Irenaeus gives no space to counterfactual hypothetical questions, such as whether God would have become incarnate had Adam not fallen.

The goal of the economy, as we have seen, is the manifestation of the glory of God in a fully living human being, partaking of the life, incorruptibility, and glory of God. But, Irenaeus asks, how can the created become a partaker of the Uncreated, unless the Uncreated first joins Himself to His creature? This necessity is decisive for Irenaeus's understanding of the economy:

> For it was for this that the Word of God was made human, and he who was the Son of God became the Son of man, that the human being, joined to the Word and receiving adoption, might become the son of God. For by no other means could we participate in incorruptibility and immortality, unless we had been joined to incorruptibility and immortality. But how could we be joined to incorruptibility and immortality, unless, first, incorruptibility and immortality had become that which we also are, so that the corruptible might be swallowed up by incorruptibility and the mortal by immortality, "that we might receive the adoption of sons"?[23]

The growth and increase that God set before the newly created being was intended to accustom that being to receive such adoption in Christ. There is no question as to whether the creatures could have accomplished this themselves if they had not apostatized.

Yet, just as we saw two aspects to the place and role of death in human existence—as catastrophic, yet embraced within a divine pedagogy—so too Christ's work is twofold: on the one hand, it renders beings animated with a breath of life into beings vivified by the Spirit, bringing them into full communion with the incorruptibility and glory of God, as His adopted sons, and new existence in the new Adam, the life-giving Spirit. The other side of Christ's work is that, as the apostatizing human race is dead "in Adam," enslaved by the devil, so Christ came to set it free:

> For he fought and conquered. For, on the one hand, he was human contending for the fathers, and through obedience doing away with disobedience

---

[23] *AH* 3.19.1 (SC 211, 374–75). Cf. 1 Cor 15:53–54; 2 Cor. 5:4; Gal. 4:5.

completely; and on the other hand, he bound the strong man, and set free the weak, and endowed his own handiwork with salvation, by destroying sin.[24]

The liberation of the human being from the tyranny of the devil is effected by Christ, who as human, fought the enemy, and loosened the disobedience through obedience, and who as God, set free the weak and gave salvation to His handiwork, doing so by voluntarily accepting that death which had no claim on Him, so manifesting His omnipotence in weakness.

As the two dimensions of the apostasy, catastrophic and pedagogic, are but a matter of perspective, so also the two dimensions of Christ's work of salvation—liberating the weak human from the devil and bestowing incorruptibility—are a matter of perspective, relating to the one Jesus Christ. Thus, while the human being, in Adam, was inexperienced and weak and so, from the beginning, easily led into apostasy, the human being in Christ, being strong, conquered the enemy by remaining obedient. Likewise, Adam was a psychical being, and, while obedient, would have remained immortal; yet he could not have become a partaker in incorruptibility, nor have been united to the Spirit, had God not united Himself to the human being in Christ. These two aspects are, of course, inseparable: they were realized by the one Jesus Christ, who is, for Irenaeus, the first manifestation of the true, fully human being.

As Eucharistic, Becoming Human

There is, for Irenaeus, one further aspect to the mystery of death, and the victory over death, when seen in the light of the mystery of Christ, and that is to see it in eucharistic terms. Irenaeus quotes the passage of St Ignatius about becoming the wheat of God:

> Suffer me to be eaten by the beasts, through whom I can attain to God. I am God's wheat, and I am ground by the teeth of wild beasts that I may be found pure bread of Christ.[25]

It is also striking how Ignatius speaks of himself as becoming human through his martyrdom:

> The pains of birth are upon me. Suffer me, my brethren; hinder me not from living, do not wish me to die. . . . Suffer me to receive the pure light; when I

---

[24]*AH* 3.18.6 (SC 211, 362–65). Cf. Rom.5:19, Matt 12:29.
[25]*Epistle to the Romans* 4:1; SC 10 (ed. Pierre Thomas Camelot; 1951), 130.

shall have arrived there, I shall become a human being. Suffer me to follow
the example of the passion of my God.[26]

Irenaeus takes the imagery further:

> Just as the wood of the vine, planted in the earth, bears fruit in its own time,
> and the grain of wheat, falling into the earth and decomposing, is raised up
> by the Spirit of God who sustains all; then, by wisdom, they come to the
> use of humans, and receiving the Word of God, become Eucharist, which
> is the Body and Blood of Christ; in the same way, our bodies, nourished by
> it, having been placed in the earth and decomposing in it, shall rise in their
> time, when the Word of God bestows on them the resurrection to the glory
> of God the Father, who secures immortality for the mortal and bountifully
> bestows incorruptibility on the corruptible (cf. 1 Cor 15:53), because the
> power of God is made perfect in weakness (cf. 2 Cor 12:9), that we may
> never become puffed up, as if we had life from ourselves, nor exalted against
> God, entertaining ungrateful thoughts, but learning by experience that it
> is from his excellence, and not from our own nature, that we have eternal
> continuance, that we should neither undervalue the true glory of God nor
> be ignorant of our true nature, but we should know what God can do and
> what benefits human beings, and that we should never mistake the true
> understanding of things as they are, that is, of God and of the human being.
> [(*AH* 5.2.3 (SC 153, 36–40)]

There is clearly a close relationship between the process that leads to the Eucharist and to the resurrection. It is by receiving the Eucharist, as the wheat and the vine receive the fecundity of the Spirit, that we are prepared, as we also make the fruits into the bread and wine, for the resurrection effected by the Word; at which point, just as the bread and wine receive the Word and so become the Body and Blood of Christ, the Eucharist, so also our bodies will receive immortality and incorruptibility from the Father. As such, death, within the overall economy of God seen in the light of the Passion of Christ, takes on a eucharistic dimension, alongside its educative and limiting function, and the economy as a whole can be described as the Eucharist of God.

"Let Us Make Man"

Irenaeus has some very particular, and rich, insights into the role of death, if we allow ourselves to make the transition from "given up" to "no, rather, gave

[26] *Ep. Rom.* 6:1–3 (SC 10, 132–34).

himself up"—to see, that is, the economy of God as one. Irenaeus's theology is also centered upon God's fashioning of the human being in a very striking manner. He is most known for his statement: "The glory of God is the living human being" [*gloria enim Dei vivens homo*: AH 4.20.7 (SC 100/1, 648)] though by this he means the martyr, the one undergoing death in confession of Christ:

> For it is testified by the Lord that as "the flesh is weak," so "the Spirit is ready," that is, is able to accomplish what it wills. If, therefore, anyone mixes the readiness of the Spirit as a stimulus to the weakness of the flesh, it necessarily follows that what is strong will prevail over what is weak, so that the weakness of the flesh will be absorbed by the strength of the Spirit, and such an one will no longer be carnal but spiritual because of the communion of the Spirit. In this way, therefore, the martyrs bear witness and despise death: not after the weakness of the flesh, but by the readiness of the Spirit. For when the weakness of the flesh is absorbed, it manifests the Spirit as powerful; and again, when the Spirit absorbs the weakness, it inherits the flesh for itself, and from both of these is made a living human being: living, indeed, because of the participation of the Spirit; and human, because of the substance of the flesh. [AH 5.9.2 (SC 153, 110–112)]

The strength of God is made perfect in weakness, and so, paradoxically, it is in their death, their ultimate vulnerability, that the martyrs bear greatest witness to the strength of God. The paradigm of the living human being is Jesus Christ Himself, and those who follow in His footsteps, the martyrs, flesh vivified by the Spirit.

If this is a living human being, then it is really only first in Christ that the work of God, announced at the beginning of Genesis—"Let us make a human being in our image" (Gen 1:26)—is now complete. There is a very significant difference between the way in which Genesis speaks of the creation of everything else and the creation of a human being. In every other case, God speaks it into existence—"Let it be"—and it was so, and it was good. But after preparing the world and everything in it, He says, "Let us make a human being in our image"—not as an injunction, but as an intention. It is in the voluntary self-offering of Christ upon the tree that Irenaeus sees the project of God finally completed, fulfilled. "It is finished," Christ says on the Cross, in the Gospel of John, just after Pilate unwittingly says, "Behold the man" (John 19:30,5). Christ is, as Irenaeus put it, "the beginning which appears at the end" [AH 1.10.3 (SC 264, 160–67); cf. AH 4.34.4 (SC 100 854–61)] Such a perspective is also present in the celebration of Holy Week in the Orthodox tradition, especially in a hymn from Holy Saturday:

Moses the great mystically prefigured this present day, saying: "And God blessed the seventh day." For this is the blessed Sabbath, this is the day of rest, on which the only-begotten Son of God rested from all his works; through the economy of death he kept the Sabbath in the flesh, and returning again through the resurrection he has granted us eternal life, for he alone is good and loves mankind.[27]

For God's intention—to create a human being—to be fulfilled requires not a divine fiat from God, for such a being would, as we have seen, be only an automaton, not freely turning to God. It requires the *fiat*—"let it be," "thy will be done"—of one able to break the bonds of death, the tyranny of the devil. But He must break this tyranny of death in no other way than by voluntarily dying, as human, so that we are all now able to give our own consent, our own fiat, to be reborn in Him in baptism, taking up His Cross, culminating in martyrdom, and so in this way ourselves become human.

The work of Atonement is not simply a once-for-all act in the past, as a discrete event following on from other discrete events—creation, fall, and incarnation. As the work of God in Christ, it is rather once-for-all in a divinely timeless manner, fulfilled in us now, by our own voluntary use of death, and inscribed within the one economy of the one God acted out by the one human race. The conclusion of *Against the Heresies* recapitulates Irenaeus's whole vision of the economy in one sentence:

> For there is one Son, who accomplished his Father's will; and there is one human race, in which the mysteries of God are wrought, "which the angels desire to see" (1 Pet 1:12), not being able to search out the wisdom of God, through which His handiwork, conformed and incorporated with the Son, is perfected; [the Father's will is] that his Offspring, the first-begotten Word, should descend to the creature, that is, to the handiwork, and be borne by it, and on the other hand, the creature should bear the Word and ascend to him, passing beyond the angels and becoming in the image and likeness of God. [AH 5.36.3 (SC 153, 464–66)]

There is one economy of the one God effected by the one Son in the one human race, embracing creation, apostasy, death and salvation, not as distinct temporal moments, but as distinct reflective moments, as we now begin to contemplate the wisdom of God manifest in the mystery of Christ.

---

[27] Doxastikon of the Stichera at Paschal Vespers on Holy Saturday; Τριώδιον Κατανυκτικόν (Athens: Apostoliki Diakonia, 1960), 431.

✝

Creation and Salvation in St Athanasius of Alexandria
Khaled Anatolios

PERHAPS THE FIRST POINT OF INQUIRY with respect to the Christian doctrine of creation is what exactly is its function within the Christian proclamation as a whole, the announcement and exposition of the good news of Jesus Christ. Is it to offer a kind of representational description of the divine act by which the cosmos came into being? Or does it attempt to depict the original state of the cosmos *after* it came into being but *before* it became disfigured by sin, and thus to analyze the being and condition of things considered in abstraction from the subsequent realities of both sin and salvation, whether one understands "subsequent" here in a temporal or merely logical sense? Athanasius's most explicit treatment of the doctrine of creation, in his early treatise *Against the Pagans – On the Incarnation*, intimates a negative response to both these alternatives.[1] For Athanasius, both the intelligibility of Christian faith and the credibility of its proclamation depend on its making sense of the only world we can possibly know, either by direct encounter or by historical memory or through the witness of revelation, and that is a world that is brought into being through divine goodness, disfigured by sin, but subject to the saving work of God that has culminated in the life, death, and resurrection of Jesus Christ. Within this framework, the proper function of the doctrine of creation within the Christian proclamation as a whole is to provide the ontological grammar for the exposition of the drama of salvation, which encompasses the entirety of human history.[2] Thus, the doctrines of creation and salvation are entirely and inseparably correlated, and it is this correlation which provides the logical structure of the great Alexandrian's two-part treatise, *Against the Pagans – On the Incarnation*.

---

[1]On the dating of this work, see Khaled Anatolios, *Athanasius: The Coherence of his Thought* (London: Routledge, 2004), 26–30.

[2]For a thorough and insightful survey of how the patristic doctrine of creation in general was closely intertwined with soteriological considerations, see Paul Blowers, *Drama of the Divine Economy: Creator and Creation in Early Christian Theology and Piety* (Oxford: Oxford University Press, 2012).

In this paper, I would like to offer some reflections on Athanasius's doctrine of creation in this treatise according to a twofold movement that aims to reflect what I consider to be the underlying logic of the work as a whole. The first and briefer part will offer a description in formal terms of Athanasius's construal of the necessary mutual correlation of the doctrines of creation and redemption in the Christian proclamation. The second part will then analyze how Athanasius's ontology of creation provides the fundamental grammar for his construal of the narrative of Christian salvation. In the course of this latter analysis, I will propose that it is precisely Athanasius's thoroughgoing correlation of the doctrines of creation and salvation that allows him to transcend any dichotomy between so-called "ontological" and "juridical" soteriologies. To further illustrate this point and to highlight Athanasius's possible contribution to the modern theological conversation, I will compare his approach to that exemplified by Fr Georges Florovsky in his famous essay on "Redemption," in which Florovsky himself seems to be engaged in overcoming a dichotomy between ontological and moral aspects of Christ's salvific work. My contention, which I trust would not have offended Fr Florovsky himself, is that Athanasius offers a more successful synthesis and a more coherent account of the Christian proclamation than Florovsky himself does precisely because he draws more directly and more comprehensively on an ontology of creation that supplies the grammar and fundamental logic of his soteriology.

1. The Mutual Relation between the Doctrines of Creation and Salvation in *Against the Pagans – On the Incarnation*

In order to appreciate the correlation of the doctrines of creation and salvation in Athanasius's *Against the Pagans – On the Incarnation*, we must first of all avoid reducing the whole double treatise to a *cur Deus homo* argument culled from the second part only, as is all too commonly done. Indeed, we must even go beyond merely tracing the logical connection that Athanasius seems to be drawing between the doctrines of creation and salvation. Rather, it is necessary to take proper account of Athanasius's explicitly stated goal, which he announces at the beginning of both parts of this treatise, and that is to provide an exposition of the Christian proclamation about the true knowledge of both God and creation which has come about through Christ. In Athanasius's own words, the subject matter is "knowledge of piety (θεοσέβεια) and the truth about the universe . . . [which] manifests itself more clearly than the sun through the teaching of

Christ."[3] The overarching claim of the whole double treatise is that this knowledge is available only through the incarnation of the Word of God, and His life, death, and resurrection.[4] It is in the service of this claim that Athanasius occupies himself with the refutation of idolatry, in the first part of the treatise, *Against the Pagans*, a fact that is otherwise difficult to explain. If this focus on idolatry seems rather passé and irrelevant to us, we should keep in mind that, considered merely as a phenomenon of human religious behavior, it was well on its way to being passé in Athanasius's own time. A significant witness of this is Athanasius himself, who tells us in this very treatise that idolatry has been largely eradicated; indeed, he presents this eradication as a major achievement of the risen Christ and as proof of His divinity.[5] Why then spend half of this double treatise in what can be considered, even in its own time, a piece of retro-apologetics?

The answer to this question lies precisely in Athanasius's understanding of the inter-relations of the doctrines of creation and salvation. For, besides being a privileged biblical paradigm for the distortion of the relationship between humanity and God, idolatry is essentially a misunderstanding of the true nature of creation, a mixing up of the categories of creature and creator. In devoting the first half of his treatise to the subject of idolatry within the larger argument that idolatry has been overthrown by Christ, Athanasius is thereby demonstrating the claim that the truth about creation is only available through knowledge of Christ, a knowledge which is itself the fruit of Christ's salvific work. Considered according to its true nature and proper relation to God as disclosed by Christ, creation is discovered to be an epiphany of Trinitarian life: "Creation itself cries out ... and shows forth God as its Maker and Creator who rules over it, the Father of our Lord Jesus Christ."[6] Athanasius reiterates this point in the last chapter of the treatise: "Having such a good Son and creator from himself, the Father did not hide him so as to make him imperceptible to the things that came into being but reveals him to all every day through the subsistence and life of the universe which he brings about."[7] Yet these affirmations of creation's

[3]Athanasius, *Against the Pagans* (*Contra Gentes*) in Contra Gentes *and* De Incarnatione (ed. R. W. Thomson; Oxford: Clarendon Press, 1971), 2. Hereafter cited as *c. gent.* All translations are my own.

[4]On the centrality of this premise to the design of the whole treatise, see E. P. Meijering, "Struktur und Zusammenhang des apologetischen Werkes von Athanasius," *Vigiliae Christianae* 45 (1991): 227–231, esp. 316.

[5]Athanasius, *On the Incarnation* (*De Incarnatione*) 55.1 in SC 199 (ed. Charles Kannengiesser; 1973), 460; cf. *c. gent.* 1 (Thomson, 1–2). Hereafter cited as *de inc.*

[6]*c. gent.* 27 (Thomson, 73).

[7]*Ibid., 47 (Thomson, 131).*

disclosure of the Father and the Son are made in the context of the argument that prior to the advent of Christ people largely did not heed the Trinitarian cry of creation (and we can also perhaps say the same in our own post-Christian context). If the ultimate meaning of creation is its disclosure of the mutual relation of the Father and the Son, this disclosure in fact only came about through the appearance of Jesus Christ as the incarnate Word and Wisdom of God. This, in a nutshell, is the essential point of the first part of this double treatise, *Against the Pagans*, which is succeeded by the second part, *On the Incarnation.*

While the necessity of the incarnation for our proper understanding of creation is implicit, albeit unmistakably so, in the first half of this treatise, the necessity for a correct understanding of creation as a *prolegomenon* to the exposition of the doctrine of the incarnation is quite explicit in the second half. In the first chapter of *On the Incarnation*, Athanasius asserts, "It is proper for us to speak first of the creation of the universe and of its maker, God, so that one may fittingly contemplate that its renewal (ἀνακαίνισιν) was accomplished by the Word who created it in the beginning. For it will appear as in no way contradictory that the Father worked its salvation in the same one by whom he created it."[8] This passage seems to support a common reduction of Athanasius's argument to the assertion that salvation requires divine agency just as much as creation did and, therefore, if Christ saves us, then He must be divine. But I would argue that the opening chapters of *On the Incarnation* initiate a much more complex logic in which Athanasius seeks to demonstrate that the Christian doctrines of creation and salvation both manifest the same rationale, which consists of certain laws of interaction, as it were, between God and creation. For Athanasius, it is precisely this consistency of rationale that provides the intelligible and persuasive content of the Christian proclamation. The doctrine of creation expresses the fundamental structure of this rationale in terms of an ontology of the inter-relation of God and creation, while the narrative of Christ's saving work becomes intelligible and persuasive precisely by manifesting its consistency with that ontology. This is why, for Athanasius, it is only the mutual correlation of both doctrines that saves the Christian proclamation from being dismissible as ἄλογον, as irrational.[9] It is also why the treatise as a whole offers an account of the intelligibility of the Christian proclamation according to a twofold movement that has the doctrine of creation as its *terminus a quo* and the doctrine of redemption as its *terminus ad quem.*

[8] *de inc. 1.4 (SC 199, 262).*
[9] *c. gent. 1 (Thomson, 2).*

2. Ontology of Creation as the Grammar of Salvation in Athanasius

I now proceed to the second and main part of my presentation, which considers how Athanasius's ontology of creation provides the logical grammar for his account of Christian salvation. I believe that the correct answer to this question will simultaneously clear up a considerable ambivalence that has arisen as to the real character of his soteriology. On the one hand, Athanasius is sometimes cited as exemplary of a supposedly Greek patristic soteriological paradigm in which we are saved primarily by the incarnation that brings about our deification, rather than by Christ's suffering and death on the Cross; and what we are saved *from* are death and corruption, rather than sin.[10] This putative Greek patristic model is often contrasted with a characterization of Western soteriology, often associated specifically with Anselm, as juridical rather than ontological, and as preoccupied with God's forgiveness of sins through Christ's suffering and death, rather than with the Word's incarnation and our deification. But on the other hand, the attempt to portray Athanasius as emblematic of a Greek patristic model, as described above, runs into embarrassing problems in confronting Athanasius's text itself, which plainly says that the death of Christ is the primary means by which Christ works our salvation and is indeed "the capstone of our faith" (τὸ κεφάλαιον τῆς πίστεως ἡμῶν)[11] and which also speaks of Christ's salvific death as annulling the penalty and repaying the debt of sin on our behalf and thereby fulfilling the demands of divine justice.[12] In fact, one finds in this classic text evidence of both an "ontological" account of salvation as well as features of a soteriology that now tends to be dismissed as "transactional" and "juridical", and which is associated with Western approaches. Indeed, I would like to suggest that Athanasius's account can make an important systematic and ecumenical contribution to current discussions of this issue precisely because of its synthesis of these motifs. Moreover, this synthesis does not consist merely in a juxtaposition

[10] Cf. R. P. C. Hanson, *The Search for the Christian Doctrine of God: The Arian Controversy 318–381 AD* (New York: T&T Clark, 1988), 450–51: "One of the curious results of this theology of the Incarnation is that it almost does away with a doctrine of the Atonement. Of course Athanasius believes in the Atonement, in Christ's death as saving, but he cannot really explain why Christ should have died. When in chapters 19 and following of the *De Incarnatione* he begins trying to explain the necessity of Christ's death, he can only present a series of puerile reasons unworthy of the rest of the treatise. The fact is that his doctrine of the Incarnation has almost swallowed up any doctrine of the Atonement, rendered it unnecessary. Once the *Logos* has taken human flesh on himself, in a sense, certainly in principle, redemption is accomplished ... Sometimes he gives the impression that our redemption is a kind of sacred blood-transfusion, or an affair of mass-transference almost independent of our act of faith."

[11] de inc. 19.4 (SC 199, 336).

[12] See *de inc.* 4, 9, and 20 (SC 199, 274–79, 294–99, 336–41).

or harmonization of alternative "models of salvation" but describes one and the same logic whereby an account of the ontology of creation supplies the grammar for articulating the proclamation of Christian salvation.

a. Athanasius and Florovsky

But before I advance to a substantiation of these claims on behalf of Athanasius, I would like to present Fr Georges Florovsky as a congenial modern dialogue partner with the great Alexandrian on these issues. In his classic essay "Redemption," Fr Florovsky himself seems to be striving toward a synthesis between ontological and moral aspects of salvation and, in the course of doing so, he cites Athanasius and other patristic theologians. It is admittedly true that Fr Florovsky does not explicitly declare any intention to forge a synthesis between moral and ontological accounts of salvation. My grounds for asserting that his essay nevertheless aspires to such a synthesis lie in the very intriguing dialectic in this essay between explaining the efficacy of Christ's salvific work in terms of His voluntary love and compassion, on the one hand, and, on the other hand, in terms of an ontology of death and resurrection. What seems to lie behind this dialectic is not so much a conscious effort to synthesize Eastern and Western frameworks, but rather, as Matthew Baker shows in another essay in this volume, a very interesting episode of intra-Orthodox dispute.[13] In the early decades of the twentieth century, Metropolitan Anthony Khrapovitsky became notorious for his vigorous refutation of Western soteriology, which also included the positive proposal that the efficacy of Christ's salvific work consisted not so much in His physical sufferings and death as in His moral suffering, His affective compassion and sorrow over every human being's entrapment by sin. It is in his apparent, though not explicit, efforts to respond to Metropolitan Khrapovitsky that we find a certain dialectic in Florovsky's account between moral and ontological accounts of salvation. On the one hand, he is quite willing to concede Khrapovitsky's assertion that the salvific efficacy of Christ's redemption resides in His voluntary and compassionate love.[14] On the other hand, Florovsky insists

[13]See Matthew Baker, "*In Ligno Crucis*: Atonement in the Theology of Father Georges Florovsky," in the present volume, pp. 101–126. See also Andrew Blane, *Georges Florovsky: Russian Intellectual and Orthodox Churchman* (Crestwood, NY: St. Vladimir's Seminary Press, 1997), 302.

[14]"A distinction must be made between the assumption of human nature and the taking up of sin by Christ. Christ is 'the Lamb of God that taketh the sin of the world' (John 1:29). But he does not take the sin of the world in the Incarnation. That is an act of the will, not a necessity of nature. The Saviour *bears* the sin of the world (rather than *assumes* it) by the free choice of love . . . He carries it freely; hence this 'taking up' of sin has a redeeming power, as a free act of compassion and love" ("Redemption," 98, italics in original).

that Christ's salvific work cannot be confined to His loving suffering or to any aspect of Christ's spiritual subjectivity. Rather, it is Christ's actual physical death that brings about His and our resurrection, which is the content of salvation. The key to the mystery of Christian salvation, says Florovsky, is therefore "a coherent doctrine of human death."[15] Thus, the ontological emphasis in Florovsky's account is preoccupied precisely with the ontology of death and resurrection and limited to just that extent. In contrast to Hellenistic dualisms of body and soul and time and eternity, he wants to show that the Christian vision asserts a more integrated anthropology in which the separation of body and soul is not natural at all but indeed constitutes the ultimate tragedy of the death caused by sin. Human death is overcome only by Christ's assuming this separation in Himself and overcoming it by the perseverance of the union of His body and soul with the hypostasis of the Word, even though His body and soul are separated from each other during the event of His human death.

Florovsky's ontological account of Christ's salvific death is valuable in itself, as is his moral account of Christ's salvific love. Yet the relation between these two approaches seems to fall short of a genuine synthesis and to devolve into a mere juxtaposition at best, which sometimes lapses into direct competition. In different places, he asserts that each of these is the primary cause of our redemption, but he also plays them off against each other. His rejection of the moral and psychological reductionism of Khrapovitsky leads him to see an ontological account of Christian salvation as somehow in tension with one that works within supposedly "moral" categories such as forgiveness of sins, reconciliation with God, and the demands of divine justice. This tension tends to be resolved consistently in the direction of relativizing what we can call the "moral drama" of Christian salvation and separating it from a supposedly deeper ontological stratum. Redemption, says Florovsky, is accomplished "not by the suffering of the Cross only but precisely by the death on the Cross. And the ultimate victory is wrought not by sufferings or endurance, but by death and resurrection. We enter here into the ontological depths of human existence … not just the remission of sins, nor merely a justification of man, nor again a satisfaction of an abstract justice."[16] In a similar vein, he elsewhere seems to depict divine justice as inferior to and dismissible by the other divine attributes of love and mercy: "Justice does not restrain God's love and mercy,"[17] and, "The Cross is not a symbol of justice, but the symbol of divine love."[18]

[15]"Redemption," 104.
[16]Ibid., 104.
[17]Ibid., 102.
[18]Ibid., 103.

Florovsky's discomfiture with so-called "juridical" approaches to Christian salvation and his privileging of a self-avowedly ontological account is paradigmatic of a prevalent strand of modern Orthodox theology, but one whose claims to consistency with the biblical and patristic witness is perhaps open to question. In his essay, Matthew Baker suggests that the dismissal of a juridical interpretation of Christian redemption is problematic and hardly consistent with the patristic witness and stipulates that "a more honest study of the language of substitution, debt-satisfaction, ransom, and law in general within patristic literature is thus in order for Orthodox theology."[19] Baker himself refers to Athanasius as an exemplar of a patristic witness to the constructive use of such language. I do not wish now simply to cite more examples of Athanasius's use of such language. Rather, I would like to propose that the lack of integration in Florovsky's soteriology, and his tendency to dismiss the role of divine justice in Christ's work of salvation, are attributable precisely to the omission of a fundamental ontology of creation that can provide a comprehensive grammar for his soteriology. In reaction to what he considered to be a moral and psychological reductionism, Florovsky was perspicacious in discerning the necessity for an ontological foundation for his soteriology. But then he made the fateful decision of turning not to the doctrine of creation for the discernment of this ontological foundation but to an ontology of death and resurrection. On the face of it, such a decision is perfectly understandable and seems apt: it places the Paschal mystery at the very heart of soteriological reflection and insists on seeing it as transformative of the human condition in the most radical way. But this foregrounding of the Paschal mystery without a supporting background in the explication of a doctrine of creation comes at a steep price. Instead of an ontology that explicates the key terms of the Creator-creation relationship as laying forth the grammar of a soteriology, Florovsky restricts himself to an ontology that is too confined to the immanentist perspective of the disintegration and reintegration of the human being in terms of the relation of matter and spirit, body and soul, and time and eternity. There is a great irony here! While asserting the Christian opposition to a Hellenistic dualism in the relation between these aspects of human existence, Florovsky nevertheless becomes unwittingly trapped in a quite Hellenistic reduction of creaturely ontology to this immanentist framework.

It is precisely in the light of this problematic and Florovsky's valiant but ultimately ambivalent engagement with it that we can appreciate the enduring value of Athanasius's distinctive structuring of the correlation of the doctrines

[19]Baker, "*In Ligno Crucis*," p. 125.

of creation and salvation. For Athanasius, too, the Paschal mystery is the very content of Christian salvation, and that content has ontological depths. But the Alexandrian bishop saw with much greater clarity that the ontological foundations for soteriology must be based on a comprehensive doctrine of creation that has centrally in view not merely the immanentist dialectics of the human constitution, but rather the negotiation of being between creatures and their Creator within the realm of moral freedom. Let us now turn to a direct consideration of how Athanasius's account of salvation derives its intelligibility from his ontology of creation and how both accounts integrate the "moral" and "ontological" dimensions of the God-world relation. If we can show that Athanasius is able to make such categories as human sin and divine justice intelligible precisely as events pertaining to the "ontological depths of human existence," we will have shown that Athanasius provides just the ontological basis for a doctrine of salvation that Florovsky was looking for, without incurring the cost of denigrating the moral, transactional, and "juridical" elements of the God-human relation.

b. Athanasius's Ontology of Creation as the Grammar of His Soteriology

Against prevalent characterizations of both patristic and Orthodox theology as emphasizing the salvific efficacy of the incarnation rather than the death of Christ, it is striking that both Athanasius and Florovsky state explicitly that it is the death of Christ which is the goal of the Incarnation.[20] We have seen that, for Florovsky, this results in a soteriology that places at the foreground an ontology of death and resurrection in which the moral categories of sin and divine justice are considered to be somehow secondary, although in a vague and undefined sense. By contrast, Athanasius grounds these moral and dramatic features of the Christian narrative of salvation in the fundamental ontological structure of the relation between God and creation, and this is what enables him to have a much more integrated synthesis of ontological and moral features of salvation. I would argue that the underlying foundation for this synthesis is an ontology of creation as gift, which Athanasius lays out in the opening chapters of *On the Incarnation*. Florovsky, along with many others, has rightly emphasized Athanasius's assertion of the contingency of creation.[21] But to hear with

---

[20] *de inc.* 19.4 (SC 199, 334); "Redemption," 96: "The Incarnation is the quickening of man, as it were, the resurrection of human nature. But the climax of the Gospel is the Cross, the death of the Incarnate."

[21] Georges Florovsky, "The Concept of Creation in St. Athanasius," *Studia Patristica* 6 [Texte und Untersuchungen 81] (Berlin: Akademie Verlag, 1962), 36–52; repr. as idem., "St. Athanasius' Concept of Creation" in *Aspects of Church History* (vol. 4 of *Collected Works of Georges Florovsky*, ed. Richard Haugh; Belmont, Mass.: Nordland, 1975), 39–62.

the right tonality Athanasius's insistence on the inherent instability and lack of self-standing that is proper to created being, we have to combine this emphasis with his equal stress that creation's being is wholly and without exception *gift*, the fruit of divine generosity. It is not creaturely contingency as such but rather divine goodness that is the primary element in the Christian doctrine of creation:

> God is good—or rather, he is the source of goodness. But the good is not begrudging of anything. Because he does not begrudge being to anything, he made all things from non-being through his own Word, our Lord Jesus Christ. Among all the things upon the earth, he was especially merciful toward the human race. Seeing that by the logic of its own origin it would not be capable of always remaining, he granted it a further gift. He did not create human beings merely like all the irrational animals upon the earth, but made them according to his own image, and shared with them the power of his own Word, so that having a kind of reflection of the Word and thus becoming rational, they might be enabled to remain in blessedness and live the true life of the saints in paradise.[22]

We can see in this passage how intertwined for Athanasius are the notions of creation *ex nihilo* and the giftedness of creation. If creation is wholly gift, then it is literally nothing apart from its "being-gifted." Moreover, this ontology of gift is also an ontology of participation.[23] The gift of being is not given to the creature in such a way that the creature can then simply walk away with this gift. Rather the content of the gift of creaturely being is ineluctably relational; it is a sharing in the very life of the divine Giver. On the human side, Athanasius's doctrine of creation also prescribes an ontology of creaturely self-determination, in which what he calls "the further gift" of human rationality includes the capacity to determine one's own being through moral choices.[24] Humanity has the power either to confirm its own being by willfully participating in the power of the divine image, or it can decline this participation and thus freely forfeit its being, sliding into nothingness and preferring the self-grasping power of sheer autonomy to the giftedness of participated being.

Athanasius's ontology of creation thus categorically asserts from the outset the co-incidence of the moral and ontological realms. Humanity's most

[22]*de inc.* 3.3 (SC 199, 270–73).
[23]On the notion of participation in Athanasius, see, further, Anatolios, *Athanasius: The Coherence of his Thought*, 50–52, 104–109.
[24]*de inc.* 3.3 (SC 199, 270).

fundamental moral choice is to either accept or reject the gift of participation in divine being, and this moral choice is thus simultaneously an ontological self-determination. Sin, therefore, not only has ontological consequences, but is itself, constitutively, an ontological event; it not only leads to but simply consists in the forfeiture of the only being that a creature can have, which is nothing else than its participation in divine life. What then of God's response to human sin in the biblical account of salvation, an account that adverts to both divine justice, as well as to mercy and forgiveness, and which includes all these within a proclamation of the salvific efficacy of Christ's death? Here again, the enduring significance of Athanasius's approach resides in his seeing all of these motifs within a synthetic conception in which the moral drama of divine-human interaction is not at all separated from what Florovsky calls "the ontological depth of human existence." [25] In contrast to Florovsky's dismissive allusion to "an abstract justice,"[26] Athanasius argues that the death of Christ is salvific in part precisely because it is a fulfillment of divine justice. Athanasius asserts that human corruptibility and death are not only the ontological contents of sin but also that they are the implementation of divine law, as pronounced in *Genesis:* "of the tree of the knowledge of good and evil you shall not eat, for in the day that you eat of it you shall surely die." (Gen 2:17).[27] God's subsequent work of salvation cannot simply abrogate this law but must fulfill it, and that is why Christ had to die in order to bring about the forgiveness of sins and our salvation: "It was absurd (ἄτοπον)," says Athanasius, "for the law to be annulled before being fulfilled."[28]

If we are inclined to denigrate the role of divine law and justice in our interpretation of Christian salvation, we can object, in Florovsky's own words, that "justice does not restrain God's love and mercy."[29] We must then put these questions to Athanasius: *Why* would it be absurd for the divine law to be set aside for the sake of divine mercy and love? Is this an abstract justice that is extrinsic to "the ontological depths of human existence"? I would suggest that the response which Athanasius implicitly gives to these question is indicated by his very suggestive description of the law as "securing the grace" of humanity's participation in God. In the context of setting forth the basic elements of an ontology of creation, Athanasius continues:

[25]"Redemption," 104.
[26]Ibid., 104.
[27]*de inc.* 3.5 (SC 199, 274).
[28]*de inc.* 8.2 (SC 199, 290).
[29]"Redemption," 102.

Knowing that the free choice of human beings could turn either way, he secured in anticipation the gift that he gave by a law and a place. He led them into his paradise, and gave them a law, so that if they guarded the grace and remained good, they would possess the life in paradise that is without sorrow or pain or care, as well as the promise of incorruptible life in heaven. But if they transgressed and turned back and became evil, they would know that they would suffer in death the corruption that is according to their nature and that they would no longer live in Paradise but would henceforth die outside it and remain in death and corruption.[30]

Reading this passage in its native context, embedded as it is within Athanasius's explication of the ontology of creation, we can glean from it that the divine law secures the gift simply by explicating the terms according to which the gift is to be received. As such, the law is neither something heteronymous to the being of creation, nor in tension with divine goodness and generosity. Rather, it is precisely a manifestation of the ontology of creation as entirely and comprehensively gift and as an expression of the divine solicitude for the integrity of that gift. Even in the ostensible mode of threat, the divine law simply announces the fundamental terms of the God-world relation within the ontology of gift by warning that the rejection of the gift of participation in divine life does not only result in but, in fact, simply consists of the forfeiture of creaturely being. A few paragraphs later, Athanasius says that salvation cannot be accomplished without death because, if it were, God would be shown to have lied in His announcement that sin will be followed by death. In the context of the entire framework of his ontology of creaturely giftedness, the point is not merely that it is inappropriate for God to go back on His word, as if God's original word was simply an arbitrary whim to which He was subsequently bound for the sake of maintaining His own consistency. Rather the word of God's law is true precisely in the sense that it is true to His creative word, true to the most fundamental and ineluctable and radically gracious terms of the relation between God and creation.

That is why Athanasius says that it is absurd for the law to be annulled without being fulfilled. We can also say that is why it is absurd for divine justice to be simply set aside in the work of redemption. Once we see the divine law and justice strictly in the context of an ontology of creation, we can understand that to annul the law and set aside divine justice would be for God to simply set aside the fundamental terms of the God-human relation. In Athanasius's framework, "absurd" is exactly the right evaluation of this proposition, since it would be

[30]*de inc.* 3.4 (SC 199, 272–75).

equivalent to saying that the God-world relation, after being broken by sin, can be restored by setting aside the God-world relation. On the contrary, Athanasius insists that the restoration of creation must be consistent with the original terms of that creation, if it is precisely that creation which is being restored. Since sin not only results in but actually consists of the ontological deprivation of death, salvation cannot simply transcend that ontological deprivation without undergoing it and reversing it from within. This is what Christ's death does.

I have noted elsewhere that Athanasius consistently speaks of Christ's death in Eucharistic language, as an offering and sacrifice.[31] Christ's death is a Eucharistic self-offering to the Father that annuls the sinful content of death as self-withdrawal from divine life. It is precisely within this framework that we must understand Athanasius's insistence that Christ's death is both a fulfillment of death and its annihilation.[32] It is a fulfillment of death because Christ enters into the place of humanity's decline into nothingness, which came about through its rejection of the gift of participation in the divine life. But Christ's death is also the annihilation of death because Christ enters into this place of withdrawal only to reverse it by His own Eucharistic self-offering.[33] Therefore, our inclusion into Christ's death of self-offering also brings about the renewal of our participation in divine life, which is resurrection. Thus, Athanasius's ontology of gift constitutes an unbroken continuum which extends from an account of creation as radically gifted, to sin and death as the creature's rejection of its own gifted being, to the death and resurrection of Christ as the eucharistic reversal of the creature's rejection of the gift of being. Hence the death of Christ is just as crucial in this account as it is in Florovsky's, yet the moral categories of human sin and divine justice are not relegated to a secondary status but instead fully integrated into a synthetic vision in which a robust ontology of creation provides the grammar for a comprehensive account of Christian salvation.

3. Conclusion:

As I intimated earlier, the subject matter of Athanasius's classic treatise, *Against the Pagans – On the Incarnation*, enfolds both the doctrines of creation and salvation within a presentation of the intelligibility and credibility of the Christian faith in Jesus as Lord. This arrangement does not leave any room for a

[31]See Khaled Anatolios, *Athanasius* (Early Church Fathers; London: Routledge, 2004), 57–60.

[32]Cf. *de inc.* 9, 20, 22 (SC 199, 294–99, 336–41, 344–49).

[33] For a fuller exposition of this point, see Khaled Anatolios and Richard Clifford, "Christian Salvation: Biblical and Theological Perspectives," *Theological Studies* 66 (2005): 756–60.

conception of the appropriate concern of the doctrine of creation as being an analysis of an original divine creative act or an original state of the effects of such an act, in abstraction from the concrete historical given of a world disfigured by sin and redeemed by Christ. Rather, for Athanasius, the appropriate function of the doctrine of creation within the Christian proclamation considered as a whole is to provide the fundamental ontological grammar for the good news of salvation through Jesus Christ. I have tried to show that Athanasius's transcendence of the dichotomies of ontological vs. juridical accounts of Christian salvation is rooted precisely in his ontology of creation. According to the terms of this ontology, creaturely being is defined as radically gifted with both a participation in divine life and the power to determine the extent of that participation through the exercise of its freedom. This ontology sets the stage for an explanation of Christ's salvific work as not only a renewal and eucharistic fulfillment of creation's reception of the gift of participation in divine life, but also as an implementation and fulfillment of divine justice in the aftermath of human sin. In Athanasius's account, the divine law which prescribes that sin must result in death is not merely the manifestation of some "abstract justice" that can simply be overruled by divine love and mercy. Rather, it is divine truth telling about the radical giftedness of creation, of which the necessary consequence is that the forfeiture of the divine gift intrinsically entails the dissolution of the creature's own being. There can be no dichotomy or tension in this account between Christ's death as fulfilling divine justice and as manifesting divine mercy and the forgiveness of sins. Sin, forgiveness, and divine justice are not relegated to some secondary status as extrinsic to "the ontological depths of human existence" but are seen as entirely determinative and constitutive of these ontological depths and of the salvific transformation of these depths brought about by the intervention of divine love and mercy. From this perspective, the salvific efficacy of Christ's death has to be explained in both ontological and juridical terms because the very gratuity of humanity's being is manifested and secured by divine law. Fr Florovsky was quite right to stress that a merely moral account of Christ's salvific work is inadequate. As I have acknowledged, he was trying in his own way to shore up the limitations of Khrapovitsky's moral soteriology with a robust ontology. If I suggest that Athanasius provides a stronger foundation for a more synthetic account of Christ's salvific work, I trust that Fr Florovsky might well have taken that suggestion as a validation of his earnest and creative commitment to the construction of a "neo-patristic synthesis."[34]

[34]For an account of Florovsky's notion of "neo-patristic synthesis," see Paul Gavrilyuk, *Georges Florovsky and the Russian Religious Renaissance* (Oxford: Oxford University Press, 2013).

✟

Theology of Salvation in St Gregory the Theologian
John McGuckin

A *Praeludium*

IF WE BEGIN, IN ACCORDANCE WITH the theme of our scholarly gathering, to look at the doctrine of atonement in St Gregory the Theologian, we must remember from the outset that the term as commonly used is not derived from the classical Greek Christian heritage of theology. Rather, it represents a sixteenth-century scholastic attempt to systematize theories of salvation, in the light of the great arguments turning around the soteriological teachings of the Church in the aftermath of the Reformation disputes. In this context the term atonement, as a clearinghouse concept, was introduced to try to get back to the heart of the matter: the way in which God reconciled with humanity in Christ. The term had two specific connotations in the theological endeavor of the Renaissance period that launched it, which I would sum up as driven by two chief concerns.

The first was an attempt to summarize, coordinate, and harmonize the disparate images and theories of salvation as presented in the Scriptures (and the classical historical tradition in which the Fathers stand), reducing them to an overriding simplicity, as discrete and contributing "aspects" of a movement to divine atonement initiated by God in Christ. To this extent the English word "atonement" is quintessentially an understanding of what the Fathers would speak of as the mystery of God's *oikonomia* of salvation, in terms of divine appeasement or reconciliation, let us say. To this day one finds a strong tendency among those who approach the mystery of salvation along the lines of "atonement" to begin with the Cross and work outward from there. This, it could be argued, is to privilege St Paul's redemption theory. But it is not as simple as that: it is actually a privileging of Romans over and against what the early Church saw as "greater Paul," particularly the cosmic hymns of redemption that we find in Philippians, Colossians, and Ephesians: most of which, modern exegetes tell us, were not by Paul, but which the Fathers had collectively subsumed as giving the wider *phronēma* of the Pauline theology of divine *oikonomia*.

The second aspect of Atonement discourse was a determination, by following this theological track, to bring back coherence into the soteriological understanding of the sacrifice of Christ. In terms of the latter idea, there was a willingness in second-generation Reformation thought to redefine Christ's sacrifice more deeply than the narrow sacramental concept that had come to dominate late medieval Roman Catholicism. This involved a return to biblical ideas of divine satisfaction, which Luther and others had lifted up as capable of bearing a profound weight as keys to the whole theology of redemption *qua gratia gratis data*. The term and organizing macro-concept of atonement, therefore, took early modern theology forward quite decisively, establishing itself almost as a "necessary" idea in Christian thought. In systematics the word still, to this day, functions as a term that primarily connotes how a theologian understands the Cross of the Lord, and how the sufferings of Jesus, in particular, establish and correlate the notions of salvation, redemption, reconciliation, and the renewal of human life. The term is very useful, but it comes at a high cost. It imposes upon the ancients a matrix of understandings that is not theirs, and also calls for a taxonomy of correlations that are not of their own making.[1] In terms of its biblical underpinnings it also substitutes a more narrowly focused range of Paulinisms in place of a wider and more capacious way of reading the apostolic heritage: the whole corpus of Paul considered as including Hebrews, Colossians, Ephesians, the Christ-Kenosis hymn in Philippians, as well as the great passages on the Cross and the victory over death in Romans and 1 Corinthians. It is against a basic premise in patristic exegesis (one formally maintained in the exegetical writings of Origen and synopsized in the *Philocalia Origenis* prepared by Basil and Gregory the Theologian), that scripture reveals its authentic exegesis only through Scripture.

In the early modern age this narrowing of the theological parameters witnessed in atonement theory was not seen as too much of a problem. Patristic theology itself was still in the process of being "coordinated" as part of the great dividing of the ways that the Reformation represented. The Anglican tradition, in particular, seeing itself as both catholic and reformed, was determined to wrest the claim to the high ground of patristic tradition from its Roman rivals. Accordingly, Anglicans made monumental and widely accessible collections of the patristic data, rivaling those prepared by the great Catholic scholars, and tried for their part to advance a systematic approach to patristic theology as a

[1]John A. McGuckin, "*Soter Theos*: The Patristic and Byzantine Reappropriation of an Antique Idea," in *Salvation According to the Church Fathers* (ed. Dirk Krausmüller and D. Vincent Twomey; Dublin: Four Courts Press, 2010), 33–44.

discrete subject. These developments gathered speed in the eighteenth century and came to a head in the nineteenth with the setting out of extensive collections of translated texts in English (efforts led by Union Theological Seminary in America and Oxford University in England), which were offered to the mainstream Protestant world as an early example of an "ecumenical" approach. The modern notion of patristic theology was born,[2] or perhaps we should say "was given a new birth" (for the concept of the authority of the fathers was an ancient one, visible in the second century and affecting the Church's canonical tradition as early as the fifth century), this time being conceived by Anglican divines largely as a form of ancient systematics. The writings of the Fathers, now considered as primarily doctrinal sources, were atomized, mined for proof texts and formulas, and taxonomically rearranged so as to provide the clearest form of a dossier of evidence. Editors and theologians of the nineteenth through the twentieth centuries actually saw themselves as "improving" on the diffuse nature of the patristic evidence.

This process is still in play: one might look, for example, to the new extensive collections of *Ancient Christian Commentary* and *Ancient Christian Doctrines*, overseen by Thomas Oden; or indeed at the majority of patrologies of the twentieth century. Two classic representations of the Reformed-Catholic approach in this regard would be Bishop Aulen's *Christus Victor* and J.N.D. Kelly's *Early Christian Doctrines*.[3] Both books, and the larger school to which they belong, have had a significant impact in laying down for modern readers the parameters of an approach to the Fathers for primary matters of soteriology. Yet both leave readers who may themselves have read extensively in the works of the Fathers (as distinct from reading the patristic florilegia these systematicians abstract for our consumption) a sense of unease as to the way in which the ancient patristic project is being represented. There is a greater willingness today to call for a more detailed examination of what the Fathers are actually saying, in their own context, and out of their own agendas, rather than reading them only insofar as we feel we can subordinate them to our systematic needs and concerns. This might leave a historical theologian with grounds for optimism; equally it could be said to leave a modern systematic theologian with significant questions as to what value the Fathers should be afforded any more.

---

[2]A concept illuminated in the recent book by Elizabeth A. Clark, *Founding the Fathers: Early Church History and Protestant Professors in Nineteenth-Century America* (Philadelphia: University of Pennsylvania Press, 2011).

[3]Gustaf Aulen, *Christus Victor: A Historical Study of the Three Main Types of the Idea of Atonement* (trans. A. G. Herbert; London: SPCK, 1931; repr. Eugene, Ore.: Wipf and Stock Publishers, 2003); J. N. D. Kelly, *Early Christian Doctrines* (London: A&C Black, 1977).

In the Orthodox tradition this is not as critical a matter as in the other western traditions, Reformed and Catholic, for the patristic evidence has for centuries been firmly lodged in the wider context of the ecclesial tradition carried by the canonical, liturgical, and ascetical evidence of the saints of previous generations. The Fathers exist as authorities in the Orthodox theological world, not mainly because they are useful evidence in the midst of controversies over doctrine or fundamental traditions, but rather because they are held to represent concrete instances of the biblical sense of the *phronēma Christou*, the mind of Christ. It is their ecclesiality that defines their patristic status, not their patristic archaic status which defines ecclesiality—a concern which has marked much of their elevation into theological debate in the West over the last two and a half centuries. As the emphasis on inter-Christian apologetics has declined in the latter half of the twentieth century, it is interesting to see how the patristic theological project has also shown a marked decline in the higher curricula, particularly in the seminaries. But I also see evidence of that decline in the movement of university religion departments, which have attempted (where they had it to begin with) to redefine the field as a subset of Classics, a secularized aspect of Second Sophistic rhetoric.

So much for a prelude as to why one cannot safely go to a patrology of the last generation and easily look up a sure guide to patristic doctrine about soteriology: because it will not exist in one place or under one systematic analogy. It is more complex than that. Basil Studer and Angelo Berardino's handbook *History of Theology: The Patristic Period* does not even mention atonement in the index.[4] Surprisingly, it does not have one for soteriology for that matter! But let this suffice as preamble. Taking the concept of atonement to mean, in regard to ancient thought, primarily how a writer understood the significance of the death and resurrection of the Lord in reference to the salvation of the human race, it will be our task now simply to review how one of the great eastern Fathers, Gregory the Theologian, wrote about the mystery of God's salvation in Christ, and to try and make some systematic deductions from that evidence at the end of our brief review.

Let us dispense with the great man's life, interesting though it be, for it can be accessed elsewhere.[5] Also, for the first time we now have many of his primary

---

[4]Collegeville, Minn.: The Liturgical Press, 1997.

[5]John A. McGuckin, *St. Gregory of Nazianzus: An Intellectual Biography* (Crestwood, N.Y.: St. Vladimir's Seminary Press, 2001); idem., "Gregory of Nazianzus," in *The Cambridge History of Philosophy in Late Antiquity* (ed. Lloyd P. Gerson; Cambridge: Cambridge University Press, 2010), 482–97; Brian E. Daley, *Gregory of Nazianzus* (Early Church Fathers; London: Routledge, 2006).

texts in translation: many of his orations in English, all of them in French, and a small proportion of his poems in modern European languages (most notably in Italian), a paucity that nevertheless represents a ten-fold increase on what was available merely fifty years ago. Even so, the poems remain an uninvestigated area, despite the important place of poetry in Gregory's theological method, as I have argued elsewhere. He had loudly signaled that a theologian had to have divine inspiration, illumination, clarity of soul and heart, and literary refinement: all of which were "proven" in the act of being capable of interpreting theology as God's herald (*kēryx*). I have elsewhere shown this claim to be a deliberate refutation of Plato's banishment of the Poet from the ideal Republic as well as Gregory's own strategy, in the face of reductionist logicians such as Eunomius and Aetius, of arguing that the theological endeavor is best defined as poetry presided over by a sensitive hierophant.[6] We neglect the poetic aspect of his project, therefore, at our own risk.[7]

Divine Anthropology: the Soteriological Dynamic of Godhead in Flesh

Several commentators of the mid- to late-twentieth century laid much emphasis on systematically dividing patristic Christology into Word-Flesh and Word-Man schools: more to their own procrustean inclinations, it has to be said, than was often merited. St Gregory the Theologian is a case in point. His Christology fits neither modality and warns us against too neat a systematician's matrix, as appears in Grillmeier's early volumes, for example. With a very strong emphasis on the full attributes of the soul of Christ, Gregory happily uses the key term *mixis*, admixture or synthesis, of the divine and human in the person of Jesus, God incarnate. St Cyril in his early Christology is deeply influenced by Gregory. Much late-twentieth-century Christological writing has presumed, wrongly in my opinion, that Cyril's early preference for *mixis* language derives from a mistaken reliance on an Apollinarist *pseudepigraphon* that he thought was Athanasian. It is much more likely that Cyril derived it from reading Gregory, and had known his works from the period when he accompanied his uncle to Constantinople in the time of St John Chrysostom's deposition. Cyril's mature opus shows that he had read extensively in the works of Origen, Didymus,

---

[6]"Gregory: The Rhetorician as Poet," in *Gregory of Nazianzus: Images and Reflections* (ed. Jostein Børtnes & Tomas Hägg; Copenhagen: Museum Tusculanum Press, 2005), 193–212.

[7]Though most editors did not care much for the poetry in literary terms, using a canon of aesthetic enjoyment for their editorial disapproval—one that Gregory himself was deliberately abandoning on the grounds that it lived up to all Plato's worst suspicions about the frivolity of poets.

Athanasius, John Chrysostom, and Gregory of Nazianzus, and thus had already, long before he realized the political necessity of the move after 433, started to augment his general reliance on Athanasian Christological thought with the Syrian streams of argument present in Gregory. The Nazianzen was a Syrian-school theologian who himself was deeply impressed by St Athanasius's centrality in the Christological debate. Cyril's *Letters to Epictetus* demonstrate this synthesis quite clearly, and in this way he opened the way for the Chalcedonian process, in which, albeit posthumously, Cyril remained a key factor. Nevertheless, in the immediate aftermath of the generation of the two Cappadocian Gregories, who posit this Christology of *synkrasis*,[8] the term was widely rejected as having only an Apollinarist connotation. Gregory's work was largely ignored, and it does not receive much attention because of a largely anachronistic scholarly understanding of what "Chalcedonian clarity" involves.

Gregory in his own day was deeply alarmed by the dyophysitism of Diodore, whom he regarded as an example of wrongly polarized thought, Apollinaris supplying for him the other wrong pole. As a result, he posited what he regarded as the golden mean between Diodoran separatism of the natures and Apollinarist confusion in a dynamic synthesis, a creative melding together of divine and human, where attributes were not lost or abrogated, but rather taken into new potentialities. The divine entered the human condition most directly, most mercifully and intimately, while the human entered into divine grace transcendently, given a new meta-physical potential allowing it to break the bonds of mortality and fleshly corruption, and ascend to communion with angelic status.

Communion was thus an important concept. It turns not merely around *koinōnia* which Gregory habitually sees as God's compassionate *synkatabasis* in the incarnate economy, but also around the central technical question of how close the Lord was to our race in His descent to earth. This, then, touches upon what we understand as the union of natures, or for Gregory the Christological *synkrasis* at the heart of the Logos' economy of salvation. For Gregory, of course, Apollinaris did *not* represent a Christology of *synkrasis* at all. For this it was necessary that two realities make a *koinōnia* in which the potentials of both were fulfilled and extended. For Gregory the principle problem with Apollinaris' ideas was that they shied away from true *synkrasis*. But in a true meeting and communion of full Godhead and full humanity, such as Gregory posited, in a singularity of subject,[9] if the divinity was not extended ontologically, being perfect, it was

---

[8]See Jacques Liébaert, *La Théologie de l'Incarnation* (Paris: Éditions du Cerf, 1966), 158–162.

[9]As Gregory elegantly and succinctly puts it, Καὶ εἰ δεῖ συντόμως εἰπεῖν, ἄλλο μὲν καὶ ἄλλο τὰ ἐξ ὧν ὁ Σωτὴρ (εἴπερ μὴ ταὐτὸν τὸ ἀόρατον τῷ ὁρατῷ καὶ τὸ ἄχρονον τῷ ὑπὸ χρόνον), οὐκ

nevertheless extended dynamically, that is, economically or philanthropically. It was enabled by its own flesh to enter into an intimate philanthropic *synkatabasis* with humanity, which thus made salvation in Christ powerfully and newly effective on the face of the earth. Humanity, on the other hand, by this *synkrasis* of natures, was indeed lifted up to new metaphysical potentials. These had been stolen from it by the ontological collapse under Adam, thereby bringing it into a metaphysical *stasis* of corruptibility and death that inevitably followed upon its moral decline from God. New humanity in Christ was capable of an immortal transcendence. Gregory's key and preferred terms for this concept of transcendence that Christ brings to suffering human nature are firstly his doctrine of *theōsis* and secondly—a theme closely related to the former—his doctrine of the admission of the human *nous* into the Holy of Holies of the heavenly temple after its earthly purification. This was a liturgical advancement into the eschatological mystery presided over by the work of Christ, the redeeming high priest of our race, who alone has the right to stand in the Holy of Holies of the divine presence, and there takes our nature with Him, *contra naturam.*[10]

For Gregory, Apollinaris was a terrible theologian precisely because he did not allow for this *mixis* and transformation to happen, but rather represented a telescopic collapse of the humanity, and its diffident "lifting up," as it were, into a divine ambit that subsumed it. This was not divine condescension, the *synkatabasis* which the scripture talked about as God's stooping down to Israel with the leading reins of mercy, but rather a somewhat standoffish holding out of a pole to a defiled humanity that the deity refuses to take into solidarity, fearful of being contaminated by it. This prurient theology, for all Apollinaris's concern to mount a theory in defense of the honor of the Divine Logos, is not actually Christian soteriology at all, but rather a projection of Hellenistic ideas about divinity as a caste apart. The Apollinarist ontology is deeply Hellenistic and mythological, not biblical or soteriologically motivated.

ἄλλος δὲ καὶ ἄλλος· μὴ γένοιτο, in *Epistle* 101.20 (*To Cledonius*) in SC 208 (ed. Maurice Jourjon; 1974), 44; echoing Origen: "In the first place, we must note that the nature of that deity which is in Christ in respect of His being the only-begotten Son of God is one thing, and that human nature which He assumed in these last times for the purposes of the dispensation (of grace) is another" (*De Principiis* 1.2.1 in SC 252 [ed. Henri Crouzel and Manlio Simonetti;1978], 110; trans. Frederick Combie, *On First Principles*, ANF 4 [1885, 1995], 246).

[10]Both approaches I have elaborated in previous studies namely: John A. McGuckin, "The Vision of God in St. Gregory Nazianzen," *Studia Patristica* 32 (1996): 145–152; idem., "Deification in Greek Patristic Thought: The Cappadocian Fathers' Strategic Adaptation of a Tradition," in *Partakers of the Divine Nature: The History and Development of Deification in the Christian Tradition* (ed. Michael J. Christensen and Jeffery Wittung; Madison, N.J.: Farleigh Dickinson University Press, 2006); and idem., "Gregory of Nazianzus," 482–97.

Yet, for all his brilliant intellect, Gregory was not actually motivated to attack Diodore and Apollinaris until they trod on his toes during the time he was working at Constantinople between 379 and 381. This reflects a recurring aspect of his rhetorical persona, as an ecclesiastical personality who habitually sought to reconcile parties on the basis of friendships and lacked the "edge" of other significant fourth-century church party leaders. The great Nicene leaders of the first phase who had survived Athanasius, i.e. Meletius of Antioch and Eusebius of Samosata, had written to Gregory the Theologian after Basil's death calling him to go to Constantinople to begin an apologetic war with the Apollinarist party there, which was ready for the opportunity to impose candidates in the soon-to-be contested see of the imperial city. Meletius meanwhile was relying on the support and help of his young protégé Diodore. While Meletius lived Gregory refused to utter any criticism of Diodore. But after Meletius's death and Gregory's ascent as archbishop of the imperial city and president of the Council of 381, Diodore quickly turned against him for three primary reasons: his initial support for the Apollinarist candidate Vitalis, against Diodore's explicit condemnation; his refusal to endorse Diodore's own "Two Sons" Christology; and finally his attempt as conciliar president to introduce a two-fold endorsement of *homoousion* language into the Constantinopolitan Creed: namely the consubstantiality of the Son as the model of that of the Spirit. Hemmed in by Diodore's alienation of the Syrian faction against him, Gregory had no choice but to resign from the council, and ever afterwards believed that the creedal failure to affirm the *homoousion* of the Spirit was a major lapse. His last works are dedicated to the "correct" interpretation of the creed's relatively vague pneumatological clauses, as meaning nothing less than the Spirit's consubstantial status with the Father and the Son.[11] In these final works, he also turns his pen caustically against Diodore's Christology as being both separatist and defective.

Diodore had failed the test of loyalty that determined with whom one was in communion: betraying friendship put him out of communion with Gregory and thereby made his doctrine open to critical analysis. *Syngeneia* mattered in

---

[11]Affirming the status of the Spirit through the category of co-doxology that had been heavily pressed by the Pneumatomachian party (it was also their preferred way to avoid ascription of the ὁμοούσιον of the Son, by allowing the Son's status also to be carried by co-glorification). The Emperor Theodosius strongly advocated the reconciliation of the thirty or so Pneumatomachian bishops at Constantinople in 381, which Gregory resisted along with the proposed conciliar decree: see *De vita sua* 1707–8 (PG 37:1148–49). His own (effective) deposition and the subsequent departure of the Pneumatomachians anyway, demonstrated the failure of the compromise attempt that the silence over the Spirit's ὁμοούσιον represented in the conciliar creed.

theology. The ties of kin and affinity clearly motivated Gregory's choice of target. In his *De vita sua* Gregory admits to his readers that it was primarily to attack Apollinarism that he was invited by leading Syrian hierarchs to make a theological campaign in the capital city in 379.[12] What he does not say, but must have been equally obvious to the Syrians, therefore, is that Gregory had deliberately disobeyed this commission and decided to attack Heterousianism instead, while at the same time apparently encouraging Vitalis, the Apollinarist party's episcopal candidate for intrusion into Antioch (whose statement of faith Gregory endorsed while at Constantinople, thereby trying to align himself with Pope Damasus).[13] His decision in Constantinople, however, to prepare a dossier of orations against the Heterousiast Arians who had taken up residence in the city, hoping to profit from the advantage provided by the death of the Emperor Valens, must have seemed a deliberate rebuff to the Antiochenes of Diodore's party.[14] It must also have seemed a decided preference for the determination of the family of Basil (Gregory of Nyssa and the deacon Evagrius Ponticus) to make suitable return for the posthumous slanders that Eunomius of Cyzicus, then resident in Constantinople, had recently launched against Basil's memory.

What turned Gregory of Nazianzus forcibly against Apollinaris, again, was not so much the theological peculiarities, which he could forgive as long as the party was stalwartly Nicene, but the fact that Apollinaris, too, had in Gregory's mind deeply betrayed friendship. While Gregory was at Constantinople, he replied to the local Cappadocian bishops, who were calling on him to resume paschal baptisms for the town of Nazianzus, that he had never been appointed to his father's see, but had only occupied it to help him. Word of this rather elastic view of the canons got around. Apollinaris, who often sent ascetical disciples to contest vacant sees and install bishops of his own party, heard the rumors that Gregory was not intending to come back to Nazianzus, and decided to target the see as a potential gain. Gregory, who actually owned the church buildings at Nazianzus and was local magistrate there, heard late in the day from his priest Cledonius that the Apollinarists were well into the process of having their own

[12]*De vita sua* 609f. (PG 37:1071).

[13]He lived to regret this when the Apollinarists targeted his own see and accused him of pneumatological heterodoxy; and also when Damasus subsequently attacked his legitimacy on the throne of Constantinople—at the same time that Diodore realized he had no friend in Gregory and started agitations against him at the Council of 381. But *Epistles* 101 and 102 do reveal that he once had friendly relations with Vitalis when the latter first set off to "claim" Antioch (in defiance of Meletius himself). Further see McGuckin, *St. Gregory of Nazianzus*, 389.

[14]See *Orations* 27–31. In Frederic W. Norris, ed., *Faith Gives Fullness to Reason: The Five Theological Orations of Gregory Nazianzen* (Supplements to Vigiliae Christianae 13; Leiden: Brill, 1991).

ascetics popularly acclaimed, and furiously gave instructions to his local clergy to see off the intruders.[15] From that time onwards, he felt Apollinaris deserved no further respect. His rancor at the attempt to place a new bishop under his nose in Nazianzus caused him to examine in detail the theology of the movement, and he tells us (retrospectively, in the *De Vita Sua*) that he did not like what he found. Much of this is rueful hindsight of course, for he wrote that poem in 383 or 384, near the time (in 385) when he was writing to Theophilus of Alexandria (via the latter's deacon Cyril) to request a synodical censure of Apollinarism, while also petitioning the Emperor Theodosius to legally proscribe the Apollinarists wholesale.[16] His famous *Epistles* 101–102 to Cledonius set out the theological reasons why the Apollinarist movement has lapsed from a true standard of faith. To these texts we should add Gregory's *Oration* 22 as a significant anti-Apollinarist Christological statement. The Theologian, as is well known, posits in the Cledonius letters the fundamental principle of Christ's humanity being a true and complete one. He argues with great clarity that Christology, and the anthropology it assumes, must always be soteriologically assessed—a principle we would do well to remember in modern thought. He, typically, digests this in axiomatic form (speaking of the soul of Christ): "What is not assumed is not saved."[17] What is less well known, perhaps, is that he is quoting Origen of Alexandria here, for the phrase derives from Origen's treatise *Dialogue with Heraclides*.[18]

Origen's theory of how the soul of Jesus was the mediating and key factor in the communion of the Logos with incarnate historical existence was something that Gregory had noted,[19] but he moderates the Alexandrian theologian considerably in his own Christological synthesis, learning much from both Athanasius and from the Syrian Church's style of heavily historical exegesis. While he is indebted to Origen's cosmic scheme of soteriology, which sees the Incarnation as the *anakephalaiōsis* that heals the whole race, this does not involve him in some of the allegorical and speculative excesses of his mentor. For Origen this

---

[15]Gregory, *Epp.* 101 and 102 (SC 208); McGuckin, *St. Gregory of Nazianzus*, 388–89.

[16]This was achieved in 383 with the Law of 3 September: see *Codex Theodosianus* 16.5.12, *Theodosiani libri XVI cum constitutionibus Sirmondianis* (ed. Paul Krüger and Theodor Mommsen; Berlin: Weidmann, 1904–1905; repr. Hildesheim: Weidmann, 2000), 1.1:859–60. See McGuckin, *St. Gregory of Nazianzus*, 390.

[17]*Ep.* 101.32 (SC 208, 50). Further see: Anna-Stina Ellverson, *The Dual Nature of Man: A Study in the Theological Anthropology of Gregory of Nazianzus* (Acta Universitatis Upsaliensis; Uppsala: Almqvist & Wiksell International, 1981) and Kenneth Paul Wesche, "The Union of God and Man in Jesus Christ in the Thought of Gregory of Nazianzus," *SVTQ* 28, no. 2 (1984): 83–98.

[18]See McGuckin, *St. Gregory of Nazianzus*, 390–93.

[19]*De Principiis* 2.6.1–5 (SC 252, 308–21).

stooping down of the Logos to communion with the "inhominated" Great Soul Jesus gives him the basis for the elaboration of the great technical language of *enanthrōpēsis*.[20] It is an iteration of Christology that stresses the reality of the two natures of divinity and humanity and also gives a strong role to the soul of Christ in effecting the spiritual vitality of the pedagogical mission of the incarnate Logos. But this Christology had many defects. Gregory of Nazianzus's rehabilitation of the Origenian scheme of soteriological incarnation constitutes a reprise of Athanasius's and also Gregory Thaumaturgus's traditions, the latter being those of his ancestral church. It removes the speculations about the separate and pre-existing Great Soul Jesus and yet retains Origen's language about the assumed man and about the state of the incarnate Lord as being a composite reality (σύνθετον χρῆμα).[21] Origen's insistence that this assumption of humanity is also the basis for a metaphysical *anakrasis* and *henōsis* of deity and humanity resulting in the *theopoiēsis* or deification of our race is also forcefully sustained by Gregory in his own work.[22] All this served to provide a strong basis for assessing the competing Christological theories of his day.

On the Sacrifice of Christ

St Gregory sees the Cross of the Lord as a key manifestation of the larger principle behind the entire *oikonomia* of the Lord's salvation of the world, effected by His divine condescension (*synkatabasis*) to the cosmos as healer and restorer of the fallenness of our race: His recapitulation of the whole of humanity. This recapitulation begins in His joining together divinity and humanity in a profound communion, but it reaches a sharp and fierce point in the motive for that union (Gregory does not shy away from the word *mixis*), which is always and at every point the healing of the race. So, the coming of the Lord into humanity is precisely to meet it at its most suffering and wounded aspect, its enslavement to death.[23] The divine συγκατάβασις, therefore, is precisely a stooping down to the lowest

[20] *Contra Celsum* 3.14 in SC 136 (ed. Marcel Borret; 1968), 38–41.

[21] Origen, *Commentary on John* 1.28 in *Commentarii in evangelium Joannis*, Origenes Werke 4, Die greischischen christlichen Schrifsteller 10 (ed. Erwin Preuschen; Leipzig: Hinrichs, 1903), 35–36; idem., *Contra Celsum* 1.66 in SC 132 (ed. Marcel Borret; 1967), 258–65.

[22] See Peter Martens, "Divinization," in *The Westminster Handbook to Origen of Alexandria* (ed. John A. McGuckin; Louisville, Ky.: WJK Press, 2004), 91–93 and J. N. D. Kelly, *Early Christian Doctrines*, 155–157.

[23] See the excellent discussion of Gregory's soteriological principles in Donald F. Winslow, *The Dynamics of Salvation: A Study in Gregory of Nazianzus* (Cambridge, Mass.: Philadelphia Patristic Foundation, 1979); also Verna Harrison, "Some Aspects of Saint Gregory the Theologian's Soteriology," *GOTR* 34 (1989): 11–43.

point of divine humility, that very point where humanity has fallen into the crisis of death and most needs the mercy that the divine condescension brings.[24]

Gregory's doctrine of the Cross is throughout heavily based on St Paul.[25] He uses the paradoxical concept of an emptying-out of glory from the Philippians hymn of *kenōsis* and describes it as God's self-humbling before the altar of sacrificial love.[26] His argument with the Heterousian theologians seizes on the point that they find the ascription of suffering and death to Christ, if He is considered as divine and consubstantial with the Father, a terrible "injury" to the dignity of the Godhead. For Gregory this "cause of dishonor" is actually cause for the greatest glorification from the Church (a point in which Cyril will follow him most powerfully). The humility of God is not a shame, but a source of wonderment and glory, that the Lord Himself should stoop so mercifully to repair the pain of death.[27] Gregory himself wonders how the Arians can have missed the central mystery of salvation, according to the teaching of the Apostle in Philippians, that it is Christ's very *kenōsis* that is the cause of His exaltation to glory.[28] Basing himself on the apostolic declaration that the Cross remains to his day a scandal to the Jews and mere folly to the Gentiles, he adds, "And let the heretics too, talk on until their jaws ache; but even so," he insists, it is the passion of the Christ that "justifies us and effects our return to God."[29]

Although the Lord did not assume sin when He entered into a fully human life, He nevertheless made the commitment to become human solely in order to heal sin.[30] This is why, although sinless, He chose to become sin. Once again following Paul, Gregory says that in assuming sin as a sacrificial victim, Christ nailed it to the Cross.[31] In assuming this weight of sin, like the scapegoat of the ancient sacrificial cult, He Himself became the "curse," but it was solely in order to destroy the effect of the curse on the rest of us, a curse that had pulled down the whole of humanity into the dust of mortality.[32] Being laid in the grave, subject to death, whose power had seized Him as a member of the fallen race, the Lord rose again from the grave, showing that death had lost its power over Him. In Christ's resurrection death itself was conquered.[33] The Cross is metamor-

[24]*Or.* 29.20 (PG 36:100c–101c).
[25]Especially the apostolic "recapitulation" synopses set out in Col 1:15–22 and Rom 5:10–21; cf. Col 2:14, Gal 6:14, Eph 2:16, Heb 12:2.
[26]*Or.* 37.3 (PG 36:285b), on Phil 2:6–11.
[27]Ibid. 37.4 (PG 36:285c).
[28]Ibid. 38.14 (PG 36:328b).
[29]*Or.* 37.4 (PG 36:285c). Cf. 1 Cor 1:23–24, Eph 2:16, Rom 4:24–5:1.
[30]*Orr.* 30.21 (PG 36:132b), 37.1 (PG 36:284a), 38.12 (PG 36:325b), 45.13 (PG 36:641b).
[31]Ibid. 43.64 (PG 36:581a), following Col 2:14.
[32]Gal 3:13; *Orr.* 2.55 (PG 35:465b), 30.5 (PG 36:108c); cf. *Ep.* 101.61 (SC 208, 62).

phosed into the supreme symbol of victory. The idea that this process thereby marks a transference for the believer, out of enslavement to death and into the principle of life, is already established by the Apostle quite clearly in that nexus of Pauline texts which are at the basis of Origen's and Gregory's own transference theory of redemptive justification.[34] They work out of this fundamental catena of biblical doctrine. Death, being expended in the body of Jesus, has lost its power in the body of those who are incorporated into Christ's new humanity, His Church. In an important aspect of that Pauline nexus, however, the image of personification, what we might call the hypostatization of death, brings in the figure of the devil who is presented as "lord of death" to Christ's role as Lord of life and victor: "Since therefore the children share (*kekoinōnēke*) in flesh and blood, he himself partook of the same nature (καὶ αὐτὸς παραπλησίως μετέσχε τῶν αὐτῶν) that through death he might destroy him who has the power of death, that is, the devil, and deliver all those who through fear of death were subject to lifelong bondage."[35]

Origen had once surmised that the ransom, mentioned in the Pauline text, had to be paid to someone: who could it be other than the Evil One who had acquired rights over fallen souls (mankind) because of their desire to sell themselves into sin? Origen's exegesis played on this notion of ransom to Satan, in a way that became popular with later patristic preachers.[36] Gregory of Nyssa's rhetoric famously developed this image in the form of the "ransom theory" of salvation: Christ's death as a form of payoff to the "one who held the dominion of death." In Gregory of Nyssa it is a double image—first the famous "fish-hook metaphor,"[37] but also an image based on the metaphor of taxation. Sin leads to

---

[33]*Or.* 29.20 (PG 36:101b); cf. Rom 6:9–10, 1 Cor 15:26 and 54–55, and 2 Tim 1:10.

[34]Phil 3:10–11, Col 1:21–22, Heb 2:9.

[35]Heb 2:14–15.

[36]Christ buys back our freedom from Satan at the price of His own blood (Origen, *Homilies on Exodus* 6.9, *Homiliae in Exodum*, Origenes Werke 6, GCS 29 [ed. W.A. Baehrens; Leipzig: Teubner, 1920], 199–201); He tricks Satan in the transaction of buying us back (*Commentary on Matthew* 16.8, *Commentarium in evangelium Matthaei*, Origenes Werke 10.1, GCS 40.1 [ed. Erich Klosterman; Leipzig: Teubner, 1935], 489–501); He comes to earth incarnate so as to correct the disorderly rule of the angelic forces (*De Principiis* 3.5.6 in SC 268 [ed. Crouzel and Simonetti; 1980], 228–31); while He is visibly bound to the Cross, at this moment invisibly it is the devil and his angels who are really bound to it (*Homilies on Joshua* 7.3 and 8.3–4 in SC 71 [ed. Annie Jaubert; 1960], 202–5, 222–27).

[37]Christ's flesh is the bait on the hook of His divinity. Satan seizes the flesh as his "right" as lord of this world, but finds he has illegitimately taken also the divinity which he could not see; the latter catches him like a sharp hook, and turns him from predator to prey. Gregory of Nyssa may well have gotten this image from his recently deceased brother Naucratius, an avid fisherman who met his death in a river while engaged in such work.

a debt necessitating redemption. This would have resonated well with his late Roman listeners—the extent of matters concerning fiscal taxation in the letters of all the Cappadocians is quite noticeable, and the frequency with which they as rhetoricians and priests had to intervene for their townsfolk was not inconsiderable. But already Gregory of Nazianzus sees the dangers of the metaphor, its very vividness allowing it to gain momentum and distract from the point of the Apostle in this instance, which is to assert that the real holder of the *kratos*, the brute force of death, is not Satan at all, but the one who wrests it from his hand, namely Christ the victor over death.[38] To that extent, Gregory the Theologian rightly sees that to be faithful as an exegete of the text of Hebrews, one sometimes has to diminish the actual details in order to allow the original picture to shine out more accurately. It is a small, but significant, instance of the art of biblical exegesis, which Gregory practices without being ostentatious, or writing any extensive commentary on a given book. The Theologian feels so strongly that this ransom theory might gain an undeserved eminence (it obviously already had) that he explicitly attacks it in *Oration* 45:[39]

> It is worth our while examining a point of doctrine which is overlooked by many, but seems to me to deserve some scrutiny. For whom was that great and wondrous blood of God shed? And why was it poured out from our high priest and sacrifice? Admittedly we were held in captivity by the devil, having been sold under sin and having abdicated our happiness in exchange for wickedness. But if the ransom belongs exclusively to the one who holds the prisoner, then I ask again: to whom was it paid? And why? If one imagines that it was paid to the devil, then how disgraceful that a robber should receive not only a ransom from God, but even a ransom consisting of our very God; and that so extravagant a price should be paid to his tyranny before he could in all justice spare us![40]

---

[38]See further McGuckin, "Soter Theos."

[39]Herein he shows his ability to distance himself from Origen when he believes that the Alexandrian does not maintain a proper balance. Origen had made a deliberate antithesis between the *Logos* considered as great angel of light, and Satan considered as chief angel of darkness. Gregory the Theologian supports neither the antithesis, nor the angelic Christology on which it stands. He is also able to distance himself from his younger colleague Gregory of Nyssa. The latter had somewhat disappointed him in the events of the Council of 381, because he had not fully supported the Theologian's insistence on introducing the ὁμοούσιον of the Spirit into the creed, preferring as he did to maintain the Basilian discretion on this point in the cause of reconciling the Homoiousians of Cappadocia to the Nicene cause.

[40]*Or.* 45.22 (PG 36:653).

With some gentle mockery he goes on to demonstrate that the "ransom" of our salvation was not a hostage fee acknowledging any rights the devil had over the race, but a sacrificial gift offered by the Son, a gift of His obedience, given in honor of the Father alone, to the Father alone. The devil held humanity in bondage as a mere jailer, not as a lord with *jus dominionis*. The Father received the offering of the sacrificial blood, not because He Himself demanded a payment to assuage His anger, but rather because it was fitting that humanity be freed in the humanity of God, liberating His own people as unconquerable victor. Dominion of life and death, belongs to those who have and hold it. The devil held it illegitimately. Christ demonstrated this in the power of the resurrection, showing the impotence of Satan's *kratos*, in that he could not keep the gates of death intact. No price ever needs to be paid to a conquered and illegitimate warlord.

Gregory's insistence that the correct exegesis of ransom theory in the biblical tradition needed to be purified from the sense of "debt owed" and returned to the original sense of a sacrifice of thanksgiving is perfectly in accord with the way the notion figures in other New Testament passages,[41] and again shows Gregory as a careful and insightful exegete. The root Pauline imagery of the conquest of death in 1 Cor 15:21–27 is before Gregory's mind here, of course, and in this central apostolic passage, Gregory correctly senses that what matters in the atonement conceived as *victoria mortis* or *redemptio servitudinis* is the core celebration of the divine power flashing out over the world. Satan is not the lord of death, paralleled to Christ as the Lord of Life, but, on the contrary a mere villainous jailer, whose fabrics are shattered by the victory of the Son's obedience on the Cross. Romanus the Melodist most beautifully encapsulated this theology in the time of Justinian when he wrote his kontakia on the despoliation of hell.[42]

In short, Gregory argues that the idea of Christ's death as a ransom is a partial rhetorical analogy that really illustrates the wider movement of the economy of God's salvation in Christ: a movement that necessitated the Son assuming human life to renew it, even at the cost of His own suffering. This losing of the self in the suffering concomitant to lapsed humanity becomes in the generosity of the person of the Son of God a veritable offering of glory to the Father, a true stooping down in compassion to the human race, lifting up all humanity in its embrace and reconciling it to God in the person and work of the high priest

[41] 1 Tim 2:6, 1 Pet 2:18.

[42] *Kontak.* 25–28, in *Sancti Romani Melodi Cantica: Cantica Genuina* (ed. Paul Maas and Constantine A. Trypanis; Oxford: Clarendon Press, 1963), 187–222.

of our race. Gregory thus takes a very firm step towards asserting the wider perspective of biblical interpretation against an excessive reliance on particular aspects of the Pauline imagery. At times, using language that bridges the Old Testament sacrificial vocabulary, yet also would have had resonances with those who were versed in Paul and even with Hellenistic members of his literary circle who recognized him as a Christian priest, Gregory speaks of the sacrifice of Christ on the Cross as "a ransom which releases us from the power of sin, when the Lord offers Himself in our place, in order to cleanse the entire world."[43]

Conclusions

Our conclusions, albeit from such a short and partial review of some of the main texts, would be the following. Gregory has indeed reflected extensively on the nature of the life-giving sufferings of the Lord of Glory. In the main he has followed the lead and suggestions of Origen. But he demonstrates his own mind by carefully returning to the dossier of Pauline references to the death of Christ. He then deliberately intrudes into the debate by arguing for a broadly-based exegesis of the whole *phronēma* of the Apostle, instead of a focus on random imagery that potentially elevates "atonement theories" that are peripheral to the main dynamic of his theological vision, which is that the Word assumed our human nature in order to heal it. He assumed it body and soul, He assumed it in a humble self-emptying, offering to the Father, not a debt of pain to be paid to an offended master, but rather a sacrifice of obedience, which turns into a sacrifice of glory offered by our race's high priest, to the Father alone. Never, ever a penal substitution. In part, Gregory's theological agenda was possibly "turned" in this direction by the need to answer important objections to Diodore of Tarsus and Apollinaris of Laodicea on his part. When left to his own devices, he much preferred to employ the imagery of *theopoiēsis* and the ascent of the human nature to the vision of God beyond its mortal fallen limitations, as being better and more cosmically reverent interpretations of why the Lord appeared among us in the flesh, and why He suffered—as our beloved healer, priest, and pedagogue.

---

[43] *Or.* 30.20 (PG 36:132a).

✠

Atonement in the Ascetic Fathers
Alexis Torrance

T HE ENGLISH WORD "ATONEMENT," as has been pointed out, is occasion-
ally used to translate *katallagē* from the New Testament. The more usual
translation is "reconciliation." Florovsky used both words when he discussed the
topic, but preferred another: redemption. Whichever word we use—atonement,
reconciliation, or redemption—we are concerning ourselves with the salvation
of man, the union of the human with the divine, which, in any Christian "model
of atonement," must have the crucified and risen Christ at its center as "author
and finisher" (cf. Heb 12:2). When we turn to the ascetic fathers, depending
on our background, we might at first be tempted to question the possibility of
discovering much, if anything, of worth on this issue in their writings. We might
wish to dismiss the corpus of ascetic writings because of its relative lack of theological speculation or elaboration, or we may simply associate the ascetic fathers
with a kind of high-flown legalism, moralism, or "works righteousness," which,
if anything, is inimical to the doctrine of the atonement. I hope to demonstrate
that neither of these positions does the ascetic fathers justice.[1]

The ascetics whom I will discuss correspond roughly to those described
in Florovsky's work *The Byzantine Ascetic and Spiritual Fathers* (thus, primarily Greek-speaking ascetics from Anthony to John Climacus).[2] There are, of
course, myriad other possible ways of interpreting "the ascetic fathers," but I
will keep to the more representative and uncontroversial names in the history
of Eastern Orthodox spirituality.

Along with setting limits to the breadth of my presentation, I should likewise set limits to its purpose and depth. Florovsky, in his article "On the Tree

---

[1] The latter approach, which caricatures the ascetics as slaves of self-love, was exemplified by
Anders Nygren, whose work *Agape and Eros* (trans. Philip S. Watson; London: Westminster Press,
1953) continues to color the perception of early Christian asceticism in the West, particularly
amongst Protestant theologians. Fortunately, more attentive and sympathetic treatments now
exist, pre-eminently Peter Brown, *The Body and Society: Men, Women and Sexual Renunciation in
Early Christianity* (New York: Columbia University Press, 1990).

[2] See Georges Florovsky, *The Byzantine Ascetic and Spiritual Fathers* (vol. 10 of *Collected Works
of Georges Florovsky*, Vaduz, Liechtenstein: Buchervertriebsanstalt, 1987).

of the Cross," is at pains to differentiate two sides of the atonement in patristic thought:

> One has to distinguish most carefully between the healing of nature and the healing of the will. Nature is healed and restored with a certain compulsion, by the mighty power of God's omnipotent and invincible grace—one may even say, by some "violence of grace." The wholeness is, in a way, forced upon human nature.[3]

The human will, on the other hand, cannot be forced in this way, and while all will be resurrected and be subject to Christ's kingly rule:

> each must justify that resurrection for himself. This can be done only in a free communion with the Lord. The immortality of nature, the permanence of existence, must be actualized into the life of the Spirit.[4]

It is especially important to note this distinction between the atonement of nature and the atonement of the will in approaching the ascetic fathers. In the preceding papers, the emphasis has rightly been placed on the first, on the manner in which the all-encompassing redemptive work of Christ is understood in the Orthodox liturgy, the Gospel of St John, St Irenaeus, St Athanasius, and St Gregory the Theologian. These papers and their content should be taken as a presupposition for this one, which will focus more on the second aspect of the atonement, the healing of the will—in other words, the personal "entering into," or appropriation of, Christ's universal atonement in the individual Christian's life.

In what follows, I will outline three facets of the appropriation or actualization of Christ's salvific atonement in the individual believer according to the ascetic fathers. The first is the centrality of right faith in Christ crucified and of baptism into Him as the non-negotiable cornerstones of the believer's reconciliation and redemption. The second is the playing out of personal atonement, the revelation of the baptismal gift, through following the way of the Cross, which is for the Christian a way of patient repentance. The third facet involves the concept of intercessory atonement: the idea that as Christ died for us, the ascetic should likewise lay down his life for his brethren (cf. 1 John 3:16), and in so doing, is given to share intimately, even creatively, in the mystery of Christ's loving and all-sufficient work of atonement.

---

[3] Georges Florovsky, "On the Tree of the Cross," *SVSQ* 1 (1953): 25.
[4] Ibid., 29.

1. Right Faith in Christ, and the Sacrament of Baptism

For those who worry that the ascetics marginalized the work of Christ through their emphasis on self-discipline, St John Climacus (a seventh-century abbot of Mount Sinai) summarizes the ascetic position: "Even if we endure ten thousand deaths for Christ, even so we shall not repay all that is due. For the blood of God is one thing, and the blood of slaves another, according, that is, to dignity, though not according to substance."[5] Climacus is making the point that ascetic labor cannot achieve any kind of salvation in itself, and that in order to have worth, all Christian struggle must be founded on the principle of the redemptive blood of Christ, whose human blood can justly be called the blood of God.[6]

A basic correct faith in Christ—both in His person and His work, taken together—was considered essential for the effective pursuit of the ascetic life. When Climacus alludes, in his practical guidance, to the two natures of Christ and blameless belief in the Holy Trinity, he is considering these a prerequisite for right ascetic practice.[7] Heresy, according to the ascetics, destroys the foundations of the Christian life. According to Climacus, even the most humble, self-deprecating, and obedient monk can legitimately disobey if "the Faith is called in question," since, as he says later, heresy cuts off access to Christian humility.[8] Again, in the letters of the sixth-century ascetics Ss Barsanuphius and John of Gaza, it is advised that if an elder is accurately determined to be a heretic by several other elders, then, and only then, should his disciples transfer their obedience to another elder.[9] The reasoning behind these warnings against heresy is eminently practical and is well described in an apophthegm of Abba Agathon:

> It was said concerning Abba Agathon that some monks came to find him having heard tell of his great discernment. Wanting to see if he would lose his temper they said to him "Aren't you that Agathon who is said to be a fornicator and a proud man?" "Yes, it is very true," he answered. They resumed, "Aren't you that Agathon who is always talking nonsense?" "I am." Again they said "Aren't you Agathon the heretic?" But at that he replied "I am not

---

[5] *The Ladder of Divine Ascent* (hereafter *Ladder*), Step 23.10–11 (PG 88:968d).

[6] The phrase "blood of God" is by no means original to Climacus: it first appears in patristic literature in Ignatius of Antioch, *Epistle to the Ephesians* 1:1 in SC 10 (ed. Pierre Thomas Camelot; 1951), 68.

[7] See *Ladder*, Step 1.5 (PG 88:633b); Step 6.1 (PG 88:793bc); Step 27.42–43 (PG 88:1117a); Step 28.18 (PG 88:1137a).

[8] *Ladder*, Step 25.6 (PG 88:992b); Step 25.17 (PG 88:996b).

[9] *Letter* 537 in SC 450–451 (ed. François Neyt et al; 2000–2001), 680.

a heretic." So they asked him, "Tell us why you accepted everything we cast at you, but repudiated this last insult." He replied "The first accusations I take to myself for that is good for my soul. But heresy is separation from God. Now I have no wish to be separated from God."[10]

As noted above, while orthodox belief was necessary, it did not need to be an elaborated faith. In some cases, of course—pre-eminently with St Maximus the Confessor—it was, but for the sake of space, I will not deal with the exceptions.[11] The concern of the ascetics we are drawing on here was, above all, putting belief into practice. This is why I have suggested that we take the previous papers as a presupposition for the ascetics: these were the beliefs about Christ and His work that grounded and guided them as they sought the personal atonement of their own will with the will of God. Before seeing how this was worked out, however, another foundational element of personal atonement for the ascetic fathers must be underscored: the sacrament of baptism.

The main context for ascetic elaborations on the importance of baptism was the Messalian controversy. Although various errors were ascribed to this amorphous group, whose name stems from the Syriac for "those who pray," perhaps their chief transgression was to deny the efficacy of baptism as a true and salvific regeneration, laying the emphasis instead on the effort of individual prayer as the sole means to sanctification and salvation. Marcus Plested has done excellent work on the theology of baptism developed by the ascetic Macarius (or Macarius-Symeon), and other notable ascetics of the period, in response to the Messalian threat.[12] Here I will focus on the concept of baptism in the work of St Mark the Ascetic, a fifth-century monk who was perhaps the most forceful and thorough of the ascetic fathers in his approach to baptism.

St Mark conceives the underlying tenet of the Messalian movement as a gospel of self-salvation (or salvation by works), distorting the Christian life so as

---

[10] *Apophthegmata Patrum*, Agathon 5 (PG 65:109c).

[11] Florovsky is my precedent here, since St Maximus is not included in his volume on the ascetics. For a recent and excellent treatment of Maximus's ascetically-minded theology, see Nikolaos Loudovikos, *A Eucharistic Ontology: Maximus the Confessor's Eschatological Ontology of Being as Dialogical Reciprocity* (trans. Elizabeth Theokritoff; Brookline, Mass.: Holy Cross Orthodox Press, 2010).

[12] *The Macarian Legacy: The Place of Macarius-Symeon in the Eastern Christian Tradition* (Oxford: Oxford University Press, 2004). On Messalianism more generally, see also Columba Stewart, *"Working the Earth of the Heart": The Messalian Controversy in History, Texts, and Language to A.D. 431* (Oxford: Clarendon Press, 1991) and Daniel Caner, *Wandering, Begging Monks: Spiritual Authority and the Promotion of Monasticism in Late Antiquity* (Berkley, Calif.: University of California Press, 2002).

to place the source of its vitality and fruits not in Christ, but in human effort.[13] The kernel of his response lies in an insistence on the perfection and completeness of baptism, which freely redeems, obliterating both the person's own sins and the curse of death inherited from Adam. This was a direct confrontation to the Messalian view that in baptism what occurred was at best a "shaving" of the evils attached to one's being (and by no means a complete uprooting of them). The consequent claim for Mark is that the fullness of divine grace is accorded in baptism, but is only revealed through the keeping of Christ's commandments—and that not because of any individual merit, but because such a way agrees with the divine will.

Baptism is the foundation of the Christian life for St Mark, but at the same time it contains that life's fulfillment. This paradox is expressed by St Mark through a distinction between the presence of grace μυστικῶς (secretly or mystically) within the baptized person and its manifestation to human experience ἐνεργῶς (actively) through keeping the commandments. As he writes, "All that have been baptized in an orthodox manner have received the whole of grace secretly, but they afterwards receive full assurance through the keeping of the commandments."[14] The distinction allows Mark to safeguard the concept of baptism as in itself an all-encompassing renewal in Christ and by Christ, while leaving room for the conscious experience of that renewal in concert with the spiritual development of the person. In doing this, he countered the Messalian equation of grace with spiritual feeling, and strove instead for an understanding of grace's perceptibility as merely an uncovering of Christ's baptismal gift already bestowed freely from on high.[15]

Such an understanding of baptism in the ascetics is essential to their vision of personal atonement. Emphasizing baptism in this way was a safeguard against

[13]Mark never names his Messalian foes, and it is difficult to discern whether he has in mind specific people or, as with many defenders of orthodoxy, is simply attacking a threatening idea (namely, in this case, that a person's effort in prayer was salvific in itself). This idea, in an embryonic form at least, certainly circulated widely, but seems rarely to have been held in its "integrity," that is, with the kind of implications that Mark deduces.

[14]*On those who think to be justified by works* 85 in SC 445 (ed. Georges-Matthieu de Durand; 1999), 156. Mark gives perhaps the most direct and comprehensive summary of his teaching on baptism at *On Baptism* 5 (SC 445, 324–48), though, of course, the whole treatise is relevant.

[15]For Hausherr, the equation of grace with spiritual feeling was the Messalians' "fundamental error": Irénée Hausherr, "L'erreur fondamentale et la logique du Messalianisme", *OCP* 1 (1935): 328–60; rpr. in *Études de spiritualité orientale* (Orientalia Christiana Analecta 183; Rome: Pontificium Institutum Studiorum Orientalium, 1969), 64–96. For a detailed overview of the ἀποκάλυψις of baptism in the life of the believer, from the angles of καθαρισμός, ἐλευθερία, and ἐνοίκησις, see Kallistos Ware, "The Sacrament of Baptism and the Ascetic Life in the Teaching of Mark the Monk," *Studia Patristica* 10 (1970): 441–52.

ever attributing salvation to oneself as a personal achievement. The fruits of Christ's work of redemption were bestowed through baptism, not on account of personal merit. And yet this could never result, for the ascetics, in mistrust for, let alone abandonment of, virtue. True virtue, revealed through the evangelical commandments and the perfect example of Christ, was rather seen as the normal and expected *habitus* of the baptized person. Baptism was precisely an inauguration into the life of the commandments, which was perceived as the authentically free life. To affirm baptism but deny the commandments was considered, as we shall see, an insult to, and even a renunciation of, baptism and the giver of baptism, Christ Himself. We come, then, to our second point, on the playing out of personal atonement in the ascetic fathers.

2. Personal Atonement: the Cross and Repentance

In this section, on a subject which could fill many volumes, I will concentrate on two interrelated themes related to personal atonement, which are in turn most clearly associated with Christ's atonement in the sources: the theme of the Cross, and that of the commandments (especially repentance). In order to introduce the ascetic approach I have in mind, allow me to quote a lengthy but representative passage from Abba Isaiah of Scetis, which brings together all the themes that concern us.

> Affirming them, that they might not be discouraged in tribulations, [Christ] put joy in the hearts [of his disciples] saying, "You are they which have continued with me in my temptations, and I appoint unto you a Kingdom, as my Father has appointed unto me; that you might eat and drink at my table" (Luke 22:28–30). He does not say this to all, but to those who have stood aright with him in temptations. Who are then those who have stood aright with Jesus in temptations, if not those who have resisted vices contrary to nature to the point of cutting them off? This is why he told them these things as he set out for the cross. Thus, may he who wishes to eat and drink at his table walk with him towards the cross; the cross of Jesus is, as it were, abstinence from all passions, to the point of cutting them off; for the beloved Apostle, having cut them off, dared to say: "I am crucified together with Christ: it is no longer I that live, but Christ who lives in me" (Gal 2:20). It is thus in those who have set at naught the passions that Christ lives. The Apostle says, in exhorting his children: "Those who belong to Christ Jesus have crucified the flesh with its passions and lusts" (Gal 5:24). Writing to

Timothy his child he said, "If we have died with him, we shall also live with him; if we endure, we shall reign with him; if we deny him, he also will deny us" (2 Tim 2:11–12). Who are those who deny him, if not those who fulfill their own fleshly will, and who insult holy baptism? For it is by his name that we were given remission of sins, and it is because of envy that the enemy enslaves us anew by sin. Our savior Jesus Christ, knowing that his wickedness is great since the beginning, gave us repentance until our last breath. For if there were no repentance, no one would be saved.[16]

Abba Isaiah speaks of the passion of Christ (the atonement proper), but relates it immediately to the practical life of the Christian (Florovsky's "atonement of the will"). The Cross of Christ must be appropriated by the disciple in order to overcome his or her own fallen will, passions, and desires. If this path of the cross is not embraced, the Christian makes a mockery of his or her baptism. In order to protect us from such a calamity, we need to repent until the end of our lives.

The choice of expressions, scriptural citations, and themes in this passage is characteristic for ascetic literature. Whenever the passion or the Cross is mentioned, it is almost always related to the ascetic's struggle to endure for Christ's sake, to obey his spiritual father, to abandon worldly desires, and so on. I will limit myself to a few examples: St Mark writes, "I call 'cross' the bearing of afflictions which come our way"[17]; St Hyperechius says, "The obedient monk will stand with confidence beside the Crucified, since on the Cross the Savior was obedient unto death"[18]; St Barsanuphius writes to one monk, "To renounce oneself and take up the cross is to cut off one's will in everything, and not consider oneself anything"[19]; St John Climacus declares, "Blessed is he who mortifies his will to the end, and leaves the care of himself to his director in the Lord: for he will be placed at the right hand of the Crucified"[20]; and finally Elder Zosima:

> You, miserable one, for one single affliction, one single humiliation, weave a thousand thoughts, setting traps for yourself like the demons. Indeed, what can the devil do more to such a soul that does this to itself? We see the Cross of Christ, every day we read of the sufferings he endured for us, and

[16] *Asceticon* 16.125–130; in French, *Recueil ascétique* (Spiritualité orientale 7bis; trans. Hervé de Broc; Bégrolles-en-Mauges, France: Abbaye de Bellefontaine, 1985), 140–41.

[17] *On Repentance* 6 (SC 445, 234).

[18] *Exhortation to Monks* 139 (PG 79:1488a).

[19] *Letter* 257 (SC 450, 224).

[20] *The Ladder* Step 4.53–54 (PG 88:704d).

we do not support even the least affliction! Truly we have forsaken the right path.[21]

The association of the Cross with endurance, the renunciation of the will, and obedience is a common ascetic trope, based in the New Testament, but it should be emphasized that this association does not imply that the ascetics supplanted the objective importance of the Cross through this emphasis on monastic virtues. St Mark the Monk is particularly clear on this point: "The commandments themselves," he explains, "do not destroy sin, for this has been done through the cross alone,"[22] and again, "Do not seek the perfection of the law [of liberty] in human virtues, for it is not found perfect in them. Its perfection has been hidden in the Cross of Christ."[23] The Cross, in other words, must always be considered the source of redemption, "not just a symbol," as Florovsky says, "but the very power of salvation, the 'foundation of salvation.'"[24] The Cross is also, as the second quotation from St Mark makes clear, the axis about which the ascetic pursues his personal atonement.

So far, I have mentioned the general idea of the cross for the ascetics and its significance for the outworking of salvation, especially insofar as it represents the pattern of endurance for each ascetic life. But the Cross as source of the remission of sins and redemption bore another significance for the ascetic fathers: it was the gateway to repentance. In order to have a proper sense of how personal atonement was conceived in the ascetics, we must turn to the summative virtue of *metanoia*.

St Nilus of Ancyra writes: "Prior to the Cross the meaning of repentance was hidden and anyone who tried to say something about it could easily be convicted of speaking rashly and inadequately. After the crucifixion, however, its meaning became clear to all, for it had been revealed at the appointed time through the wood."[25] Similarly, St Mark declares that before Christ's sacrifice "there was no means for repentance, there being no priest without stain."[26] Repentance here—*metanoia*—signifies a redemptive about-face, a salvific change of mind and of heart towards God. This is not simply a specific act for the ascetics, but a *mode of life*, one inaugurated through the Cross, and gifted in the sacrament of baptism. As we saw in Abba Isaiah, repentance must continue

---

[21]*Conversations* 5b (PG 78:1688d–1689a).
[22]*On Baptism* 3.43–46 (SC 445, 310).
[23]*On those who think to be justified by works* 29 (SC 445, 138).
[24]Florovsky, "Tree of the Cross", 17, citing St John Chrysostom.
[25]*Ascetic Discourse* 30 (PG 79:760a).
[26]*On the Incarnation* 31 in SC 455 (ed. Georges-Matthieu de Durand; 2000), 286.

until one's last breath. For St Mark the Ascetic, the whole Christian life could be reduced to this one idea. He eloquently expresses his thought on the matter in his treatise *On Repentance*, which opens as follows:

> Our Lord Jesus Christ, the power and wisdom of God, foreseeing for the salvation of all what he knew was worthy of God, decreed the law of liberty by means of various teachings, and to all set a single goal, saying: "Repent," so that we might understand by this that all the diversity of the commandments is summed up by one word: repentance.[27]

Against the Novatians, who doubted the efficacy of repentance after baptism for grievous sins, St Mark presents his concept of continual repentance. He argues in part via a particular reading of Heb 6:1–6 and 10:26 (a reading shared, it should be said, with John Chrysostom, Ambrose of Milan, and Theodoret of Cyrrhus), on the impossibility of restoring (or renewing) the apostate again "unto repentance" (*eis metanoian*).[28] The purpose of these verses is by no means, Mark insists, to question the validity or possible frequency of post-baptismal repentance. The impossibility of a second "renewal" and "enlightenment" mentioned in the Epistle does not signify the impossibility of a second repentance, he says, but of a second baptism. He uses this platform to argue that baptism is the basis of authentic repentance, that which enables it. He can thus declare that "in all our activity, there is but one foundation of repentance—and that is the one baptism in Christ."[29]

Repentance, or personal atonement, was for the ascetic fathers a matter of response to the gift of Christ. The sacrifice of the Son of God contained the salvation of the world, and its grandeur was always the source and the spur for Christian ascetic practice. As St Dorotheus of Gaza exhorts, "Let us sacrifice ourselves, let us give ourselves over to death daily, as all the saints have done, for Christ our God, for Him who died for us."[30] Such was the basic attitude towards personal atonement in the ascetics. Before moving on to our third and final point, I would like to highlight that this kind of approach to personal atonement, permeating the spirituality of the East, is not altogether foreign to the recent divines of substitutionary atonement. A few lines from a remarkable

[27] *On Repentance* 1.1–7 (SC 445, 214).

[28] *On Repentance* 7–8 (SC 445, 234–44). Cf. Ambrose, *De Paenitentia* 2.2 in SC 179 (ed. Roger Gryson; 1971), 134–40; John Chrysostom, *Commentary on Hebrews* 9.4 (PG 63:80); Theodoret of Cyrrhus, *Commentary on Hebrews* 6 (PG 82:717bc); Mark the Monk, *De Paenitentia* 7 (SC 445, 236–38). See also Ephraim the Syrian, *Commentary on Hebrews* 6 (ACCS: NT 10, 84–85).

[29] *On Repentance* 7.25–6 (SC 445, 238).

[30] *Instructions* 16.168 in SC 92 (ed. Lucien Regnault et al.; 2001), 462.

book by the Presbyterian theologian William Douglas Chamberlain will serve as a fitting close to this section:

> I believe that the New Testament teaches the substitutionary atonement, but there are reaches of thought in the atonement that none of the doctrines formulated by men have yet explored. Too often the substitutionary atonement has been accepted in the spirit of "Jesus paid it all, so there is nothing for me to do." As I understand the atonement in the light of 2 Cor 5:15, Jesus paid it all, so I owe my all to him.[31]

The last sentence succinctly summarizes the mindset of the ascetics.

3. Intercessory Atonement

The ascetic quest for personal reconciliation with God through the pursuit of the way of the Cross inevitably brought up the relationship between the reconciling Cross of Christ and the personal cross of the ascetic. For the ascetic fathers, one's personal cross was not meant to stop at the self. As a following of Christ and an entering into the mystery of His death, it was likewise an entering into the mystery of intercession. The most striking context in which this intercessory atonement is described is in the relationship of spiritual father and child. St Barsanuphius of Gaza, though protesting his unworthiness, again and again would take on the burdens of his disciples, considering it an essential ingredient of true spiritual paternity. He boldly interprets several New Testament passages referring to the Son as applicable also to the spiritual father:

> Each of the saints, bringing before God his sons whom he has saved, will say with a loud voice, with great assurance ... "Here I am, I and the children God has given me" (Isa 8:18; Heb 2:13). And not only will he hand them over to God, but himself also, and then God will be "all in all" (cf. 1 Cor 15:28).[32]

In this way, Christ's atonement is, as it were, appropriated by the ascetics. This is justified on the basis of the commandment of love: "'Strive for your neighbor as for yourself' (cf. Lev 19:18), says the Old Testament, but the New, demonstrating perfection, enjoins us to lay down our lives for each other (cf. 1 John 3:16), just as the Perfect and Son of the Perfect laid down his life for us."[33] By

---

[31] *The Meaning of Repentance* (Philadelphia: The Westminster Press, 1943), 147.

[32] *Letter* 117.22–7 in SC 426–427 (ed. François Neyt et al.; 1997–1998), 448; cf. *Letter* 187, in the same volume.

[33] *Letter* 484.12–6 (SC 451, 592–94).

following this path, St Barsanuphius can declare that "gladly and with much ardor I sacrifice myself for your souls, as God knows, who alone knows our hearts."[34] Such an attitude is considered natural in one who repents sincerely, thereby growing in love. Indeed, St Mark explicitly articulates this form of self-giving love in terms of a perfected repentance: "The saints are obliged to offer repentance for their neighbor, since without an active love it is impossible to be perfected."[35] Elsewhere, he gives an incisive comment on the role of the ascetic who has attained dispassion (*ho apathēs*: literally, one who is free from passion or suffering): "Do not say that a dispassionate person cannot suffer affliction; for even if he does not suffer on his own account, he is under a liability to do so for his neighbor."[36] The evangelical summons to "follow in the steps" of Christ (cf. 1 Pet 2:21) has no limits for the ascetics. Personal atonement, which Christ never needed, could hardly exhaust for them the idea of living as Christ lived. The summit and goal of personal atonement always had to be the reconciliation of the other. "A true shepherd," writes St John Climacus, "shows love, for by reason of love the Great Shepherd was crucified."[37] And again, "We can offer no gift to God so acceptable as to bring Him rational souls through repentance. The whole world is not worth so much as a soul."[38]

Before concluding, let me end this point with another passage from St Mark, on standing surety or acting as sponsor (*anadochos*) for one's neighbor. "The sponsoring that comes from love is that which the Lord Jesus transmitted to us."[39] Having taken on all our sufferings, and death itself on the Cross, "to his own apostles he passed on this law, as to the prophets, fathers, and patriarchs: the latter being taught before by the Holy Spirit, the former being shown the example through his immaculate body."[40] The essence of this teaching and law is encapsulated, says Mark, in the words "no one has greater love than the one who lays down his life for his friends" (John 15:13).[41] This law was perpetuated by the apostles who taught that "if the Lord laid down his life for us, we also should lay down our lives for the brethren" (1 John 3:16) and that we should

---

[34]*Letter* 111.10–2 (SC 427, 436). Cf. *Letter* 57.55–6 (SC 426, 282): "I gladly give my life to the death for you, my brother"; and *Letter* 353.17–19 (SC 450, 374): "Remember this, brother, that, as you know, I gladly give my life for you, and my prayer for you is unceasing."

[35]*On Repentance* 11.15–17 (SC 445, 250).

[36]*On those who think to be justified by works* 123 (SC 445, 166).

[37]*To the Shepherd* 5 (PG 88:1177b).

[38]*To the Shepherd* 13 (PG 88:1196d).

[39]*Conversation with a lawyer* 20.5–6 (SC 455, 84).

[40]*Conversation with a lawyer* 20.21–4 (SC 455, 84).

[41]*Conversation with a lawyer* 20.27–29,60–63 (SC 455, 84–88).

"bear one another's burdens, and so fulfill the law of Christ" (Gal 6:2).[42] The atonement, then, for the ascetics, was a dynamic reality that called, above all, for participation and cooperation. By living out his personal atonement and reconciliation through repentance, the ascetic was grafted into the work of Christ for the salvation of all. In this sense, he perhaps had no need of our models of atonement, having come to know and live the mystery "from the inside."

Conclusion

Florovsky began his work on the *Byzantine Ascetic and Spiritual Fathers* with a pointed and rhetorical question:

> If the monastic ideal is union with God through prayer, through humility, through obedience, through constant recognition of one's sins, voluntary or involuntary, through a renunciation of the values of this world, through poverty, through chastity, through love for mankind and love for God, then is such an ideal Christian? For some, the very raising of such a question may appear strange and foreign.[43]

I hope, in a modest way, to have contributed to Florovsky's cause on this issue: the ascetic approach to the atonement is, I have argued, unmistakably Christian, perhaps even discomfitingly so.

St Barsanuphius exhorts one of his disciples with a beautiful interpretation of Matt 10:14 (the sending out of the apostles, also at Mark 6:11, Luke 9:5): "Take leave of the world, mount the Cross, raise yourself from the earth, shake off the dust from your feet."[44] When we consider the atonement in the ascetic fathers, we are given to glimpse the reality of true Christian discipleship. In the act of shaking the dust from their feet in order to mount the Cross of Christ, they do indeed bear testimony against this world, but in so doing, they, in and like their Master, seek this world's atonement.

---

[42] *Conversation with a lawyer* 20.63–67 (SC 455, 88).
[43] Florovsky, *Byzantine Ascetic and Spiritual Fathers*, 17.
[44] *Letter* 48 (SC 426, 260).

✝

In Ligno Crucis:
Atonement in the Theology of Fr Georges Florovsky
Matthew Baker

OUR THEME IS SUGGESTED BY AN original typescript of Fr Florovsky, housed in the Princeton University Firestone Library archives, entitled "*In Ligno Crucis:* The Patristic Doctrine of the Atonement." This document was based on three lectures delivered in November 1936 at King's College, University of London, and again later the same month at Lincoln Theological College, where Florovsky's close friend Michael Ramsey, the future Archbishop of Canterbury, was then sub-warden.[1]

Florovsky expanded and revised the lectures many times, publishing parts of them at various occasions and also attempting now and again to turn them into a significant book. A version of that long effort appeared in 1976 under the title of "Redemption" in volume 3 of Florovsky's *Collected Works.* The original typescript, however, still tells us significant things. The Latin title, *In Ligno Crucis,* is drawn from the preface of the Mass of the Roman Rite for Maundy Thursday:

> *Qui salútem humáni géneris in ligno crucis constituísti: ut, unde mors oriebátur, inde vita resúrgeret: et qui in ligno vincébat, in ligno quoque vincerétur.*[2]

[1]Florovsky met Ramsey at Lincoln in 1932. Later in life, he would comment that he regarded Ramsey and Mascall (who replaced Ramsey at Lincoln in 1937) as "the best younger people" on the Anglican theological scene at that time: Andrew Blane and Thomas Bird, "Interview with Fr. Georges Florovsky on Nov. 8, 1969" (unpublished typescript in my possession), 83. Florovsky's handwritten notes on the cover of the 1939 typescript also mention several other significant figures of the Anglican establishment in connection with the 1936 lectures and the intended book, including E.L. Mascall, Maurice Relton, and Derwas Chitty. For Florovsky's comments on the invitation to London, see Andrew Blane, *Georges Florovsky: Russian Intellectual, Orthodox Churchman* (Crestwood, N.Y.:St Vladimir's Seminary Press, 1993), 70–71. The theme of atonement was chosen by Florovsky himself: Andrew Blane and Thomas Bird, "Interview with Fr. Georges Florovsky on Nov. 8, 1969" (unpublished typescript in my possession), 65.

[2]"Who didst place the salvation of the human race in the wood of the Cross: that whence death began life should rise, and he who once conquered through the tree should by the tree be also overcome." The passage, in context, can be found in The Daily Missal and Liturgical Manual with Vespers for Sundays and Feasts from the Editio Typica of the Roman Missal and Breviary, 1962 (London: Baronius Press, 2008), 880–81.

The title thus places the consideration of soteriology in a *liturgical* and further, specifically *eucharistic*, context. Moreover, as an Eastern theologian alluding to the classical *Latin* liturgy as an authoritative theological source, Florovsky points to a common ecumenical tradition, shared by Fathers of both East and West. The chapters of Florovsky's intended book all bear titles drawn from Church Latin, as did the original lectures[3]; the book preface also is headed with an epigraph drawn from St. Augustine: *Morte occisus mortem occidit.*[4] On a further ecumenical note, Florovsky does not hesitate to employ the term "atonement": a word with no exact Greek or Latin equivalent, introduced probably by John Wycliffe at the end of the fifteenth century, and frequently carrying Reformed theological connotations.[5]

These liturgical and ecumenical dimensions are elaborated by Florovsky himself in his preface to *In Ligno Crucis*. After emphasizing the general, introductory nature of his lectures, he states:

> One special point must be stressed here. The Patristic doctrine of the Atonement was incorporated in the Liturgy. Numerous quotations given in this book / and it would be very easy to make many more / prove that we have here not only some private speculations or *theologoumena*, but the common mind of the worshipping Church. One can best be initiated into the spirit of the Fathers by attending the offices of the Eastern Church, especially in Lent and up to Trinity Sunday. Most of the hymns and collects used to belong to the Patristic epoch. The *lex credendi*, as presented in the Patristic writings, is corroborated by the *lex orandi*. And again, this is the witness, not merely of the Eastern Church alone, but rather the Undivided Church of old, of the Church of the Fathers. One can compare it with the testimony of the early

[3]The titles of the three original 1936 lectures were as follows: (1) "Agnus Dei"; (2) "Triduum Mortis"; (3) "Totus Christus, Caput et Corpus." According to Florovsky's handwritten notes on a typescript of the 1939 preface (Princeton CO586 Box 2, folder 1), the published book was to include five chapters: (1) "Ad lectorem" (preface, 7 pages); (2) "Mysterium Mortis" (10 pages); (3) "Seminarium Mortuorum" (26 pages, plus a later extra 3 page insert); (4) "Triduum Mortis/High Priest and Victim" (17 pages); and (5) "Totus Christus, Caput et Corpus (The Last Adam)" (18 pages). The editor's decision to exclude Florovsky's own title, preface, and Latin chapter headings in the 1976 version ("Redemption") obscures the obvious ecumenical appeal of Florovsky's original essay.

[4]Augustine, In Ioann. tr. 12.10 (PL 35:1489): *ipsa morte liberavit nos a morte; morte occisus mortem occidit* (By death itself He liberated us from death; slain by death, He slew death). This text does not appear as an epigraph in the 1976 "Redemption" version, but is quoted in an endnote, coupled with citations of similar statements from Greek Fathers: cf. "Redemption," 302n110.

[5]It should be noted that this word hardly appears in Florovsky's published work, his preferred English translation for the Russian *iskuplenie* being "redemption."

Latin Church, as exhibited by St Augustine or by St Leo in his glorious liturgical sermons. And on the whole, one can describe the Patristic doctrine of the Atonement as a *liturgical* or *sacramental* theory, in contrast with any others, juridical, moralistic, or "political." In the sacramental practice and rites of the Church the dogmatic teaching finds its fulfillment and expression. And the dogma is here again the living "*kerygma*" of salvation.[6]

Liturgical-sacramental and ecumenical: we shall have to keep these crucial contexts in view as we consider the substance of Florovsky's treatment of the atonement.

The ecumenical and liturgical orientations stressed by Florovsky in his unpublished preface help us to place the essay properly within the wider scope of his thought[7] while also illuminating Florovsky's widely misunderstood critique of Westernizing "pseudomorphosis" of Orthodox theology.[8] After delivering his atonement lectures in early and mid-November 1936, Florovsky attended—at the end of the same month—the first Pan-Orthodox Theological Conference in Athens.[9] In two papers delivered there, he summarized the

[6]"Ad lectorem," 1948 revised typescript preface to *In Ligno Crucis* (pp. 140–141 in the present volume).

[7]In his 1939 preface, Florovsky describes the work as "but a pointer to what one may describe as a neo-patristic synthesis." This is perhaps the earliest evidence of Florovsky's use of the exact phrase "neo-patristic synthesis"—a phrase which does not appear in published form until the 1947 publication of "In Ligno Crucis: Kyrkofädernas Lära om Försoningen, Tolkad från den Grekisk-ortodoxa Teologiens Synpunkt," *Svensk teologisk kvartalskrift* 23, no. 4 (1947) (see translation in present volume); and, better known, "The Legacy and Task of Orthodox Theology," *Anglican Theological Review* 31, no. 2 (1949): 65–71. In "Legacy and Task," Florovsky describes the work of neo-patristic synthesis in terms of the "reintegration" of tradition, "a secure start for the healing of Christian disruption"—a task in which "Roman Catholic and Protestant scholars are already working together in various directions" and which "the Orthodox have to join in" (ibid., 70).

[8]For Florovsky, the "pseudomorphosis" of Orthodox theology meant primarily (1) alienation of "school" theology from liturgical (and ascetical) life, with consequent loss of "existential" character; and (2) *servile imitation* of foreign sources, making creative development necessary to meeting Western theology in dialogue on equal footing impossible. As Florovsky poses the ecumenical problem: "Is 'pseudomorphosis' and imitation the only possible form of meeting or the most natural one? The true meeting will only take place when the common ground is discovered": Florovsky, "The Eastern Orthodox Church and the Ecumenical Movement," *Theology Today* 7, no. 1 (1950), 78. See also: idem., "Western Influences in Russian Theology," in *Aspects of Church History* (vol. 4 of *Collected works of Georges Florovsky*, trans. Thomas Bird and Richard Haugh; Belmont, Mass.: Norland, 1975), 167–68 (based on a paper originally presented in 1936; see 157n for the various versions); idem., *Ways of Russian Theology*, vol. 1, (vol. 5 of *Collected works of Georges Florovsky*; ed. Richard Haugh; trans. Robert Nichols; Belmont, Mass.: Nordland, 1979), 36–37; and idem., "The Problem of Ecumenical Encounter," in *Rediscovering Eastern Christendom: Essays in Commemoration of Dom Bede Winslow* (ed. A.H. Armstrong and E. J. B. Fry; London: Darton Longman & Todd, 1963), 68.

[9]Florovsky's lectures at the University of London were delivered Nov. 5, 10, and 12, 1936; the

argument of his new book, *Puti russkogo bogoslovija*, completed just two months prior (on September 15, 1936, in Berkshire, England), giving a critical history of Latin and Protestant influences upon the development of modern Russian theology.[10] "Servile imitation" of these Western influences, he argued, caused a painful schism between prayer and thought, liturgy and learned theology, leading to a "pseudomorphosis" of Russian "school" theology. Noting significant examples of this schism and its resultant malformation, Florovsky mentioned the theology of atonement:

> The doctrine of Atonement is presented in our popular textbooks either according to Anselm of Canterbury or some later Post-Tridentine authority. And the typical patristic idea, so vigorously emphasized in the liturgical texts, that Christ's Resurrection was the climax and the real source of the victory over death has been completely overlooked by our theologians."[11]

Florovsky called for the purification of Orthodox theology from the accretions of Baroque neo-scholasticism, Pietism and German Idealism, and for a return to patristic and liturgical sources. Yet, in his conclusion to *Puti*, he also insisted that the way to the renewal of Church theology and mission lay not in Orthodox theologians cutting themselves off from the West, but rather *in sympathetic dialogue with Western theology on the basis of a common patristic foundation*. Further, he argued, Orthodox theologians should engage *on this basis* most especially the questions raised by the medieval Latin schoolmen.[12] Critical of Anselm and neo-scholastic influence, yet with positive appeal to Latin liturgical

Lincoln lectures shortly after. For the impressions of a Roman Catholic guest present at the Athens conference later that same month, see the essay by Christophe Dumont OP (1898–1991), one time director of the *Istina* center, "En marge du premier congrès de théologie orthodoxe Athènes 29 novembre–3 décembre 1936," *Russie et chrétienté* 2, no. 1 (1937): 55–65. See also, Blane, *Georges Florovsky*, 71–72.

[10]The two Athens essays were "Westliche Einflüsse in der Russischen Theologie," in *Kyrios: Vierteljahresschrift für Kirchen- und Geistesgeschichte Osteuropas* 2 (1937): 1–22 [English translation: "Western Influences in Russian Theology," cited above], and "Patristics and Modern Theology," *Procès-verbaux du Premier Congrès de Théologie orthodoxe à Athènes* (ed. Hamilcar Alivisatos,; Athens, 1939), 238–42; rpr. in *Diakonia* 14, no. 3 (1969): 227–232. For complete book see Florovsky, *Puti russkogo bogoslovija* (Paris: YMCA Press, 1988), which was later translated into English in two volumes as *Ways of Russian Theology* (vol. 5–6 of *Collected works of Georges Florovsky*; ed. Richard Haugh; trans. Robert Nichols; Belmont, MA: Nordland, 1979).

[11]Florovsky, "Patristics and Modern Theology," 229.

[12]Florovsky, *Puti*, 512–16, esp. 515 (*Ways*, vol. 2, 301–304, esp. 303). Florovsky noted in his later years that patristics was for him a way of talking to westerners, especially Anglicans, in terms they could understand: Andrew Blane and Thomas Bird, "Interview with Fr. Georges Florovsky on Nov. 8, 1969" (unpublished papers in my possession), 76–77.

tradition and the Fathers, most especially Augustine,[13] and in dialogue with the great medieval schoolmen on the foundation of the patristic sources and foundations: these are dimensions and tensions we need to hold together, if we are to grasp the heart of Florovsky's thinking on atonement.

Florovsky often stressed the importance of penetrating through to the *question* behind an author's affirmations. He remarked that he himself wrote to deal with *problems*, and that the Fathers should be studied to help us answer our own problems.[14] We intend the same: exploring first the major dimensions of Florovsky's own theology of redemption in light of the problems he sought to answer, and then asking briefly how his answers succeed in helping us to face our own problems.

The "Justification of Time": Redemption as Historical Event

One of the fundamental lessons of Florovsky's entire oeuvre is the truth that redemption is a unique *historical event*, taking place objectively *in time*. Redemption fulfills the purpose of creation, and this fulfillment takes place through *history*. As Florovsky stressed in an unpublished piece titled "Redemption," a précis written in the 1950s for the planned expansion of *In Ligno Crucis*, the peculiar temporality of redemption accounts also for its comprehensive scope as "an epitome of the whole of Christian doctrine":

---

[13]It was at Lincoln Theological College on the eve of WWII that Florovsky is said to have quipped, with not a little irony: "I would say that Augustine is really an Eastern Father": E. L. Mascall, "Georges Florovsky (1893–1979)," *Sobornost* 2 (1980): 69. Christoph Künkel regards this remark as indicative of Florovsky's open-ended understanding of the nature of Orthodox tradition: see his *Totus Christus: Die Theologie Georges V. Florovskys* (Göttingen: Vandenhoeck and Ruprecht, 1991), 249n422. In an unpublished 1967 lecture given at Fordham University, Florovsky referred to Augustine as "the greatest Father of the Western Church, indeed of the Church universal" (!), whose ecclesiology "is in complete conformity with that ecclesiology which one can develop on the basis of the Greek patristic tradition. Actually there is one patristic tradition" ("Images of the Church in the Greek Fathers," Lecture IV, 1, Princeton C0586, Box 4, Folder 12). On Florovsky's estimation of Augustine, see also Matthew Baker, "The Eternal 'Spirit of the Son': Barth, Florovsky, and Torrance on the *Filioque*," *International Journal of Systematic Theology* 12, no. 4 (2010): 382–403.

[14]On the priority of "questions" and "problems," see Florovsky, "Types of Historical Interpretation" [1925], in *Readings in Russian Philosophical Thought: Philosophy of History* (ed. and tran. Louis J. Shein; Waterloo, Ontario: Wilfred Laurier University Press, 1977), 89–108, at 91 and 98; idem., "Western Influences in Russian Theology," 176; idem., "The Predicament of the Christian Historian," in *Christianity and Culture* (vol. 2 of *Collected works of Georges Florovsky*; Belmont, Mass.: Nordland, 1974), 31–65, at 36–38; Blane, *Georges Florovsky*, 171; and Brandon Gallaher, "Georges Florovsky on reading the life of St Seraphim," *Sobornost* 27, no. 1 (2005), 58–70, at 62.

Redemption is an historic event, as much as it is also an eternal design. It is a sovereign deed of God, but it is also an offer to man, and man's response in faith belongs to the very structure. The world has been redeemed, once and forever, but it is still being redeemed, and is to be redeemed. Christ's coming is itself both an accomplishment, a consummation of the Promise, and an inauguration of the New Covenant, of the New Humanity, of the "New Creation." Christ and His Body, the Church, cannot be separated. Indeed, the Church is precisely the "Realm of Redemption"—to be consummated at the End of Times. The doctrine of Redemption must be presented as the History of Salvation, as *Heilsgeschichte,* in a wide perspective—from Creation to Consummation. On the one hand, we have to stress the unity of the Biblical Revelation, and this affects the very method to be used. *Novum Testamentum in Vetere latet. Vetus Testamentum in Novo patet.* In fact, basic categories of doctrinal interpretation are derived precisely from the Old Testament, although they appear in a new light in the context of the Evangelic consummation: the Messiah, the Suffering Servant, the Sacrifice, and the like. On the other hand, the full scope of the Redemption will be disclosed only in the Age to Come. And for that reason the "Realm of Redemption" has intrinsically also an eschatological dimension.[15]

This emphatic concern for the *event-ful* character of history had already marked Florovsky's earliest philosophical essays of the 1920s, before his turn to more exclusive focus on patristics and theology. Florovsky attacked Idealism for insensitivity to history, and criticized Soloviev and Florensky for the presentation of Christianity as a "religion of the Logos," cosmologically conceived, rather than of the historic Christ.[16] One must theologize historically, he argued, beginning, not from a-historical, eternal principles—the divine Sophia or *logos asarkos* before the world's creation—but from unique historical events: the incarnation, Cross, resurrection, and ascension of the incarnate God-man.[17]

By the mid-1920's, Florovsky had already begun to give central place to the Chalcedonian dogma in explicating these singular events. As he wrote in 1927:

[15]The text of the précis is published for the first time in the second part of the present volume, pp. 153–156, esp. 154.
[16]"The Weariness of Spirit: On Fr Paul Florensky's *The Pillar and Confirmation of Truth*"[1930] in Florovsky, *Philosophy: Philosophical Problems and Movements* (vol. 12 of *Collected works of Georges Florovsky,* ed. Richard Haugh; Vaduz: Büchervertriebsanstalt, 1989), 126–127; see also, *Ways,* vol. 2, 276–281.
[17]See Florovsky, "Human Wisdom and the Great Wisdom of God" [1921], in *Philosophy,* 120–121.

Christian dogma contains by way of premises, the entire metaphysics, metaphysics true and certain. The Christian philosopher has to find, define and explain these premises ... And since Jesus Christ is the principal object of dogmatic experience, it is possible to say that the entire Christian philosophy is a speculative interpretation of Christological dogma, the dogma of Chalcedon.[18]

This Chalcedonian focus Florovsky shared with Sergei Bulgakov, who was at that time his father confessor.[19] Both theologians were sensitive to the criticism of nineteenth-century liberal Protestant scholars that Chalcedon had distorted the history of Jesus with static ontological categories of nature. For Bulgakov, Chalcedon gave a "dogmatic synthesis" in the form of apophatic formulas, but in itself failed to provide positive "theological synthesis."[20] Similarly, for Florovsky, Chalcedon signaled "a new concept of 'nature'" which, however, it did not clarify, and further, it left the exact form of the "single hypostasis" unexplained.[21]

Beyond these agreements, however, one observes a conflict. For Florovsky, theological clarification of Chalcedon had already been given in Leontius of Byzantium's asymmetrical Christology and Maximus the Confessor's dyotheletism[22]; the task was to draw out implications for ecclesiology. In contrast, Bulgakov saw his own sophiology as providing the needed positive synthesis.

Bulgakov employed the Chalcedonian statement as an overarching principle in the three volumes of his trilogy *On Godmanhood: The Lamb of God, The*

[18]Florovsky, "L'idée de la création dans la philosophie chrétienne," *Logos: Revue internationale de la synthèse Orthodoxe* 1 (1928): 3–30, at 1–2 (not the same as the 1949 English article of the same name). As Florovsky would later frequently affirm: "One can evolve the whole body of Orthodox belief out of the Dogma of Chalcedon": idem., "Patristic Theology and the Ethos of the Orthodox Church," *Aspects of Church History*, 24.

[19]Letters from this time show Chalcedon as a crucial theme of their exchange: see Catherine Evtuhov, "The Correspondence of Bulgakov and Florovsky: Chronicle of a Friendship," *Wiener Slawistischer Almanach* 38 (1996), 37–49, at 40–41.

[20]Cf. Sergius Bulgakov, *The Lamb of God* (trans. Boris Jakim; Grand Rapids, Mich.: Eerdmans, 2008), 51–63, 443 *et passim*. On Bulgakov's view of the *positive*, theological elaboration of Chalcedon as the "supreme and final problem" for theology, see Paul Valliere, *Modern Russian Theology: Bukharev, Soloviev, Bulgakov* (Grand Rapids, Mich.: Eerdmans, 2000), 297–300.

[21]Florovsky, *The Byzantine Fathers of the Fifth Century* (vol. 8 of *Collected works of Georges Florovsky*; ed. Richard Haugh; trans. Raymond Miller, Anne-Marie Döllinger-Labriolle, Helmut Wilhelm Schmiedel; Vaduz, Liechtenstein: Büchervertriebsanstalt, 1987), 299.

[22]For Florovsky's interpretation of "asymmetrical" Christology and Leontius, see *Byzantine Fathers of the Fifth Century*, 270, 296–299. The original Russian differs from the English text, at times even drastically, so cf. Florovsky, *Vizantiiskie Ottsy V–VIII* (Paris: YMCA, 1933), 26–27, 242.

Comforter, and *The Bride of the Lamb.*[23] Inspired by Soloviev, Bulgakov posited a pre-existent correlation between divine and human nature within the Trinity itself—the hypostasis of the *Logos* being somehow pre-existently "human from all eternity."[24] In contrast, Florovsky read the "two natures" language of Chalcedon as marking an absolute ontological hiatus between Creator and creature, a hiatus of natures bridged, brought into a-symmetric unity only by the person of the incarnate Word, in a single synergistic activity of two wills, human and divine, within the historical economy. The "positive" elaboration of Chalcedon is therefore to be found only by interpreting the language of the "nature" in conjunction with the redemptive *work* of Christ in history. As Florovsky wrote to Bulgakov in 1926:

> I believe in your case, too, Solov'ev long hindered you in your search for the main thing. For the road to discovering it lies through Christology, not through trinitology [*sic*], since only with Jesus Christ did the worship of the trinity become reality. *The point here is that only in history, in the realm of historical experience, are we capable of understanding the creaturehood of creation.*[25]

The "main thing" here is not any pre-existent unity or eternal divine-human correlation, but a divinely initiated *historical event*. Redemption and the *telos* of creation consist in the union of God and man. Yet this union is achieved only in *history*, as a radical ontological novelty, and cannot be apprehended apart from that history's form, witnessed in the biblical narrative and given concrete continuing form in the Church, the body of Christ.[26]

This narratological emphasis is obvious in Florovsky's portrait of Philaret of Moscow, the one unquestioned hero of his deeply anti-hagiographical *Ways of Russian Theology.* Much of this work's account of Philaret is drawn from an article published almost a decade earlier, in 1928—the same period in which

---

[23]Bulgakov, Agnets Bozhii: O bogochelovechestve, I (Paris: YMCA, 1933); idem., *Uteshitel': O bogochelovechestve, II* (Paris: YMCA, 1936); idem.,*Nevesta agnysa: O bogochelovechestve, III* (Paris, 1945). Translated into English as *The Lamb of God* (2008), *The Comforter* (2004), and *The Bride of the Lamb* (2001) (trans. Boris Jakim; Grand Rapids, Mich.: Eerdmans).

[24]Bulgakov, *Lamb of God,* 188. In contradiction to Florovsky's "asymmetric Christology," Bulgakov writes: "The attempt to find such a synthesis by Leontius of Byzantium is only a formal scholastic theory with the imprint of Aristotelianism": Bulgakov, *Lamb of God,* 443–444.

[25]Translation in Alexis Klimoff, "Georges Florovsky and the Sophiological Controversy," SVTQ 49, no. 1–2 (2005): 75, italics mine; original Russian publication: "Pisma G. Florovskogo S. Bulgakovu i S. Tyshkevichu," *Simvol* 29 (Sept. 1993): 207.

[26]For a similar approach by a recent theologian, see Aaron Riches, "After Chalcedon: The Oneness of Christ and the Dyothelite Mediation of his Theandric Unity," *Modern Theology* 24, no. 2 (Apr. 2008): 199–224.

the first version of Florovsky's essay on atonement appeared. Florovsky stresses the soteriological accent of Philaret's theology, having as its primary theme the biblical history of God's covenant with man "from creation to redemption," with special attention "to the dogma of atonement as a divine revelation of holy love."[27] Philaret, he says, "always proceeded from the facts of Revelation and moved among them."[28] "A 'system' of theology was something fully dependent and derivative. History came before system, for Revelation was given in history."[29] At the heart of this history was the Cross, understood precisely in cultic, liturgical terms: "Christ is the mysterious First Priest who is offered and who brings the offering ... the Lamb of God and the Great Hierarch ... [of] the Epistle to the Hebrews."[30] As we shall see, Florovsky follows Philaret closely in this liturgical note.

But to conclude this first, most fundamental theme of Florovsky's treatment of atonement—redemption as *event*—we may cite the words from an early Florovsky piece of the 1920s:

> Christianity is the justification of time, the philosophy of creation, the doctrine of creation arising out of nothing and entering into eternity—the doctrine of its becoming eternal. In this is the significance of Christian metaphysics. And it is revealed through the contemplation of the historical Christ.[31]

It is this "justification of time" through the historic Christ that led Florovsky to oppose any thought which treated Christ's humanity and the "form of a servant" of his redeeming work as an "episode" to be surpassed on the belief that "events, as temporal happenings, have no permanent significance,"[32] there being "no room for a true historical uniqueness, for an ultimate decision, accomplished in time, by one major event."[33] This tendency he criticized not only in Origen but also much of modern theology.[34] As he observed:

---

[27]Florovsky, "Filaret, Mitropolit Moskovskii," in *Put'* 12 (Aug. 1928): 3–31, at 19.

[28]Florovsky, *Ways*, vol. 1, 217.

[29]Ibid., 212.

[30] Ibid., 217.

[31]Florovsky, "Protivorechiya origenizma," in *Put'* 18 (Sept. 1929): 108–9.

[32]"The Patristic Age and Eschatology: An Introduction," in Florovsky, *Aspects of Church History*, 72; see also "The Anthropomorphites in the Egyptian Desert," ibid., 93.

[33]"Origen, Eusebius, and the Iconoclastic Controversy," in Florovsky, *Christianity and Culture*, 110 and 112–13.

[34]On Florovsky's abiding concern for "Evangelical realism" against the docetic tendencies of Origenism, see John Fine, "Florovsky in America," *Byzantinische Forschungen* 27 (2002), 111–124. This concern leads Florovsky to underscore the continuing humanity of the ascended Jesus, stress-

Theological liberalism, at least from the Age of the Enlightenment, persistently attempted to disentangle Christianity from its historical context and involvement, to detect its perennial "essence" ("das Wesen des Christentums"), and to discard the historical shells . . . The emphasis was shifted from the "outward" facts of history to the "inward" experience of the believer. Christianity, in this interpretation, became a "religion of experience," mystical, ethical, or even intellectual . . . The historicity of Christianity was reduced to the acknowledgment of a permanent "historical significance" of certain ideas and principles, which originated under conditions of time and space, but were in no sense intrinsically linked with them. The person of Christ Jesus lost its cruciality in this interpretation . . . this anti-historical attitude was itself but a particular form of an acute historicism, that is, of a particular interpretation of history, in which the historical has been ruled out as something accidental.[35]

The Enlightenment dualism between history and truth—the "broad ugly ditch" between contingent facts of history and absolute truths of reason announced by G.E. Lessing—and solidified by Kant's reduction of atonement to an individual regeneration through a universal rational ethics not dependent upon any historical event—results finally in such moderns as Bultmann and Tillich thinking of the historic Christ as having no more than a symbolic relation to the truth of God:

> One indulges too easily in the dialectics of the Finite and the Infinite, of the Temporal and the Eternal, etc., as if they were but terms of a logical or metaphysical relation . . . There is a subtle but real docetic flavor in many recent attempts to re-state traditional faith in modern terms . . . The whole impact of the Incarnation is reduced to symbols . . . some august principle.[36]

ing the Chalcedonian ἀτρέπτως as applicable still in the state of glorification: as he wrote to Fr Sophrony Sakharov in 1958, "Christ in his ascension is no less man than 'in his days with us,' and perhaps more (on this issue Origen was very ambiguous, and something of this ambiguity remained unanswered also in late patristic theology, primarily because of the difficulty of clearly describing the 'glorification' of human nature)": Arkhimandrit Sofronii (Sakharov), *Perepiska s Protoiereem Georgiem Florovskim* (Svyato-Ioanno-Predtechenskii Monast'ir'/Svyato-Troitskaya Sergieva Lavra, 2008), 78. On this note, as well as in his sensitivity to the implications of this continuing humanity of the ascended Lord in his ecclesiology, Florovsky anticipates somewhat the arguments of Douglas Farrow, *Ascension and Ecclesia* (Grand Rapids: Eerdmans, 1999) and *Ascension Theology* (London: T&T Clark, 2011).

[35]Florovsky, "Predicament of the Christian Historian," *Christianity and Culture*, 32–33.

[36]"The Ever-Virgin Mother of God" [1949], in Florovsky, *Creation and Redemption* (vol. 3 of *Collected works of Georges Florovsky*, Belmont, Mass.: Nordland, 1976), 174.

Against such historical docetism, then, Florovsky's first, fundamental lesson regarding atonement is the truth that salvation depends not simply upon inward experience or timeless universal "principles," but on an objective historical event, wrought by the God-man in real space and time, and having permanent fructifying power throughout all history.

The Atoning Death on the Cross: Against Kantian Moralism

Florovsky often recycled his own work for new contexts.[37] Large portions of his 1936 atonement lectures were based on his 1930 Russian essay, "O smerti krestnoi [On the Death on the Cross]."[38] Together with the 1928 "Tvar' i tvarnost," this essay represents the first, most synthetic—and, in Florovsky's own view, most lasting—fruit of his patrological studies begun shortly before he became professor of patristics in Paris in 1926. In fact, Florovsky already stated as early as 1932 his intention to expand "O smerti krestnoi" into a full-length book entitled *In Ligno Crucis*.[39]

Much has been made of the implicit anti-sophiological motive underlying Florovsky's writings. A footnote in the untranslated 1930 Russian essay,[40] however, indicates that its original context was the debate over the 1917 work of Metropolitan Antony Khrapovitsky,[41] *The Dogma of Redemption*. Antony's views

[37]As Künkel has most meticulously shown: *Totus Christus*, 17–19.

[38]Florovsky, "O smerti krestnoi," *Pravoslavnaya Mysl'* 2 (1930): 148–187. Somewhat earlier, Florovsky had also given an *unwritten* address in French on "the patristic vision of the atonement" to Berdyaev's ecumenical colloquium: Andrew Blane, "Interview with Fr. Georges Florovsky on Dec. 9, 1971" (unpublished typescript, 13/172); see also George Williams, "George Vasilievich Florovsky: His American Career (1948–1965)," *GOTR* 11, no. 1 (Summer 1965): 32. Jacques Maritain, who was also a participant, notes in his diaries a meeting at Berdyaev's apartment on March 5, 1929, in which there occurred a "discussion with Florovsky about co-redemptive suffering"; Maritain remarks how "this notion surprisingly seems to elude our Orthodox friends": Jacques Maritain, *Carnet de Notes* (Paris: Desclée de Brouwer, 1965), 220. One wonders whether Florovsky's criticisms on this occasion were not in fact leveled in reaction to Khrapovitsky's concept of redemption as co-suffering love.

[39]See the July 2, 1932 letter of Florovsky to Fritz Lieb in Vladimir Janzen, "Materiali G.V Florovskogo v archive F. Liba," Issledovaniya po istorii russkoi mysli 7 (2004/2005 [publ. 2007]): 474–596, at 571.

[40]Florovsky, "O smerti krestnoi," 155–56n3.

[41]As a theologian, Florovsky regarded Khrapovitsky as "very bad . . . a left-wing modernist. And a right-wing reactionary politician," whose election as patriarch in 1917 would have been a "catastrophe." Nevertheless, Antony "was very gifted, and had some positive qualities . . . he was a charming man, and for some reason he loved me . . . I saw him only once . . . You must understand that Antony was typical of a certain generation. People were searching for what can be called a living religion . . . they wanted to feel it, it was emotional, you see. One form of emotionalism is

caused a controversy due to the objections of two exiled bishops, Theophan (Bystrov) of Poltava and Seraphim (Sobelov) of Boguchar, leading Anthony to compile (in 1924) a catechism that soon attracted the censure of the Russian Synod Abroad. Antony attacked the juridical theory then widely taught in Russian dogmatics manuals: the doctrine that we are redeemed by the merits of Christ through the satisfaction of divine justice.[42] According to Antony, justification in the New Testament had a strictly moral significance. It is Christ's co-suffering love, expressed in His moral suffering for the sins of the world in Gethsemane, which redeems. All other soteriological terms of the New Testament are relativized by this central truth.[43]

As its title suggests, Florovsky's essay "O smerti krestnoi" responds by underscoring the redemptive necessity of Christ's *death*. Redemption was accomplished "not by the suffering of the Cross only, but by the death on the Cross." It is a typical failure, Florovsky remarks, not to "distinguish clearly enough these two things: suffering and death," and an error particularly affecting Anthony. Florovsky accuses Antony of elevating Gethsemane over Calvary. One must explain Christ's death, not just His suffering; but this Anthony treats in merely moral terms: Christ hallowed the fear of death, to make it less fearful. Here, Florovsky avers, dogmatics is reduced to "psychologism."[44]

Florovsky's atonement essay should be read together with his treatment of Antony in *Ways of Russian Theology*. As he stresses there, Antony was primarily a

moralism"; A. Blane and T. Bird, "Interview with Fr. Georges Florovsky on April 4, 1969" (unpublished typescript in my possession), 25–26. All this, however, did not keep Florovsky from making occasional positive appeals to Antony in his own treatment of the themes of the Church as *imago Trinitatis* and the "catholic transfiguration of personality."

[42]Florovsky also expressed criticism of legal atonement metaphors in his earliest essays, and this critique continued to inform his later dogmatic treatment of redemption: see especially Florovsky, "O patriotizme grekhovnom i pravednom," repr. in Florovskii, *Iz proshlogo russkoi mysli* (Moscow: Agraf, 1998), 132–165, and below for discussion.

[43]Apart from Khrapovitsky, another important argumentative context for Florovsky's work on atonement is his critique of the theology of Emil Brunner. Florovsky had hoped to publish a German version of his essay, and in a 1931 letter to Fritz Lieb, he expressed his interest in knowing the opinion of Karl Barth regarding "O smerti krestnoi" specifically in relation to the Christology of Emil Brunner: see Janzen, ed., "Materiali G. V Florovskogo v archive F. Liba," 559. Comparison with Florovsky's 1928 review of Brunner's book *Der Mittler* (in *Put'* 13 [Oct. 1928]: 112–115) and certain comments on Brunner in his 1962 essay, "The Last Things and the Last Events," *Creation and Redemption*, 254, suggests also that he has Brunner in mind here in these comments from the preface to *In Ligno Crucis:* "Strangely enough these modern theories are much more abstract than was the Patristic metaphysics ... The crucifixion itself is so often interpreted less as a crucial event in time, than as a kind of symbol which had to express the ultimate condemnation of sin by divine righteousness" (140).

[44]Florovsky, "O smerti krestnoi," 155–56n3.

pastor, who placed great stock in the power of compassionate identification with his flock in aiding the moral regeneration of sinners. Antony viewed the sacrament of priesthood as a "certain intensive grace of love, 'the gift of compassionate love.'" This was linked with his theory of redemption: "Why do Christ's inner, heartfelt torments over human sinfulness manifest themselves as our redemption? Because a love that shares our sufferings united his spirit with ours, and thus we draw from the Spirit of Christ as from a spring of sanctity, thereby conquering sin."[45] For Antony, redemption resided mainly in this moral regeneration.

Florovsky's complaint is that all this leaves the death on the Cross in the shade. Further, the priesthood is eclipsed by pastorship: "The sacramental moment . . . remains completely unexpressed."[46] Anthony marginalizes even sacrifice: "The purifying blood, the saving cross, the life-bearing grave—all are only images," important for the "feeling of compunction" they elicit as aids to moral regeneration."[47] Anthony conducts the dogmas, Florovsky says, "not to spiritual contemplation," but to "'moral experience'."[48] Florovsky suggests a source for this dogmatic moralism:

> In metaphysics Antonii is much more cautious than the Holy Fathers were, and this is his weakness. He undoubtedly resembles Kant and the method of the second *Critique*. Is Antonii's "moral experience" not identical with "practical reason"? Does the justification of dogma not lie in the fact that the ideal presuppositions of virtue are realized in it? Anthony himself admits that Kant: "had an almost infallible ability to extract the practical idea from every truth of faith."[49]

[45]Florovsky, *Ways*, vol. 2, 206, quoting Anthony's 1924 *Orthodox Catechism*.

[46]Ibid., 207.

[47]Ibid., 210. In his later years, Florovsky commented on the presuppositions and practical fruits of this moralism: "Antony started by saying we do not understand dogma, dogmatics. And if there are dogmas it is because they have ethical value. This is precisely what the French modernists said—do not think it is the truth, it is ethical truth, dogma tells you something about what you should do. This is where it began. Feel with Christ in Gethsemane. Go with Him to the agony, and you are redeemed by associating yourself with the experience of Christ. This is modern[ism]. I called this in *Puti* a protestantism of the eastern rite, and modernism of the eastern rite. You keep all the paraphernalia and visible splendor and reduce doctrine to a minimum, and in that dogma is interpreted in a moralistic sense, plus this you add right wing politics, and this you have as the Synod Abroad." According to Florovsky, such "moralistic modernism" led to an emphasis upon "tipikon more than Scriptures, obedience to bishops much more than Orthodoxy": Andrew Blane and Thomas Bird, "Interview with Fr. Georges Florovsky on April 4, 1969" (unpublished typescript in my possession), 26.

[48]Florovsky, *Ways*, vol. 2, 209.

[49]Ibid., 209.

Anthony did in fact write to *refute* Kant's view that the dogmas of the Trinity and atonement contribute nothing to ethics.[50] In attempting to overthrow Kant on his own ground, however, he implicitly accepts Kant's critique of metaphysics: dogma is approached, not as *knowledge* of objective realities, but a catalyst to moral duty. Anthony "does not verify the ontological presuppositions of his teaching."[51] It is not enough "to replace an overly 'juridical' concept of satisfaction (*satisfactio*) by the more God-befitting principle of love. One must understand and explain the place of redemption on the plane of the Divine economy, as it was *objectively* realized."[52] Florovsky concludes:

> It is quite wrong to reduce the whole content of patristic theology to asceticism and asceticism, moreover, interpreted psychologically. No less characteristic for the Fathers is their metaphysical realism . . . one cannot substitute asceticism in the place of dogmatics, or dissolve dogmatics in asceticism. This temptation is always an indicator of theological decline.[53]

Just as in his struggle to assert the abiding significance of events in man's salvation, so again we see Florovsky wrestling with a fundamentally Kantian, Enlightenment problematic: the reduction of Christianity to morality, and behind that, the denial of man's ability to know the structures of events as they take place in real space and time.[54] Florovsky's crucial answer to the first plank of that problematic is to point out that redemption deals not simply with a moral problem, but with the problem of *death*.

The Saviour came to destroy death by His own death. "The ultimate reason for Christ's death must be seen in the mortality of man."[55] Redemption is the "liberation of man from the 'bondage of corruption'."[56] However, this means

---

[50]See Antony Khrapovitsky, *The Moral Idea of the Main Dogmas of the Faith* (Dewdney, British Columbia: Synaxis Press, 1984), 25.

[51]Florovsky, *Ways*, vol. 2, 211.

[52]Ibid., italics mine.

[53]Ibid., 214.

[54]In a letter to the Russian émigré literary critic Yuri Ivask, dated 11/16/1968, Florovsky commented that he regarded this moralism as no less dangerous than the Russian religious "renaissance" whose sophiological currents he himself had also opposed: "In politics, M.A. [Metropolitan Antony] was extreme right, but in theology, he was a 'modernist' who in effect sought to reduce the whole of metaphysics to morality and psychology. Berdyaev, not without reason, called him 'Tolstoy in a cassock.' What I wrote about him in *Puti'* now seems too soft. This moralistic 'modernism' is no less dangerous than the 'Renaissance'": "Iz pisem o. Georgiya Florovskogo Yu. Ivasku," *VRKhD*, 130, no. 4 (1979): 49–50.

[55]"Redemption," 110.

[56]Ibid., 109.

that "the Cross is more than merely suffering Good."[57] "The death on the Cross was effective, not [simply] as the death of an Innocent one, but as the death of the Incarnate Lord. 'We needed an Incarnate God; God put to death, that we might live'—to use a bold phrase of St. Gregory of Nazianzus."[58] Here we see Florovsky's a-symmetrical Chalcedonianism at work: as he writes, "It may be properly said that God dies on the Cross, but in his own humanity."[59]

Apprehension of the redeeming *work* therefore requires, as Florovsky would put it much later, "an accurate conception of Christ's *Person*."[60] This is in fact where Florovsky's atonement essay begins. In the incarnation, human nature was assumed into hypostatic unity with God Himself. This is the "basis of the whole redeeming work of Christ," the fundamental conception behind the Church's Christological dogma: "the Incarnation as Redemption."[61] Yet God does not redeem by a momentary fiat, but a whole life, lived in the form of a servant. Here Florovsky appeals to the Irenaean notion of recapitulation: "the Incarnation had to be manifested in all the fullness of life, the fullness of human ages, that all that fullness might be sanctified."[62] "The *whole* life of the Incarnate One was one continuous sacrifice."[63] "However, the climax of this life was his death . . . The redeeming death was the purpose of the Incarnation."[64]

The death of Christ is of necessity for salvation precisely because through it, eternal life enters the realm of death. Thus, Holy Saturday itself is "the very day of our salvation."[65] As the icons suggest, Christ enters hades as *Victor*, despoiling death. The view held by Nicholas of Cusa and in some Reformed circles, which has recently entered Roman Catholic theology through Hans Urs von Balthasar, that Christ suffered the torments of hell, Florovsky, therefore, explicitly rejects.[66] "The power of the Resurrection is precisely 'the Power of the

[57]Ibid., 99.
[58]Ibid., 132.
[59]Ibid., 132.
[60]Florovsky, "Patristic Theology and the Ethos of the Orthodox Church," *Aspects of Church History*, 27–28, italics mine.
[61]"Redemption," 96.
[62]Ibid., 97
[63]Ibid., 101, italics mine.
[64]Ibid., 99.
[65]Ibid., 139.
[66]Ibid., 141 and 304–305n121. On this theme, see also Florovsky's remarks in his March 10, 1958 letter to Archimandrite Sophrony: *Perepiska s protoiereem Georgiem Florovskim*, 45–48; a French translation of the letter can be found in Archimandrite Sophrony, "Correspondance avec le Père Georges Florovsky," *Buisson Ardent: Cahiers Saint-Silouane l'Athonite* 14 (2008): 14–21, at 16–17. Hints of a view similar to Balthasar's may be detected in Bulgakov and in Sophrony himself.

Cross,'" of which resurrection is "not only a consequence, but a fruit."[67] Here Florovsky finally resorts to the language and imagery of the liturgy: the Paschal *Triduum* of Greek and Latin traditions. Holy Saturday commemorates "the mystery of the resurrecting Cross," the descent by which, Florovsky says—citing the *synaxarion* notice from Matins on Holy Saturday—"called from corruption, our race passed to life eternal."[68] "The tree of the Cross is an 'ever-glorious tree,' the very Tree of Life . . . 'by which the lamentation of death is abolished'."[69]

Atonement as Liturgy:
The Church as Sacrament of Christ's Atoning Work

This liturgical dimension is more than just a matter of witness. According to Florovsky, atonement is itself a liturgy. Where Antony had practically eliminated sacrifice and sacrament,[70] Florovsky, appealing to Hebrews, places the high priesthood of Christ at front and center. The death on the Cross was a sacrifice, of which Christ was both offerer and offering, priest and victim. Begun on earth, it is consummated in heaven, "where Christ presented and is still presenting us to God, as the eternal High Priest." Christ's sacrifice is more than just love, but "a sacramental action, a liturgical office," offered "not only for the remission of sins, but also for our glorification."[71] Florovsky's robust appreciation of the continuing humanity of the ascended Jesus, manifested in many of his important ecclesiological essays, can be felt at work here: it is the man Christ Jesus, the one mediator between God and men, who is continually at work in His body, the Church, as the sole priest of all sacramental action.[72]

The first, 1930 version of Florovsky's atonement essay concludes with baptism. The death on the Cross is a baptism by blood, a baptism of the whole Church, cleansing all of human nature and the cosmos. Sacramental baptism images and participates in this one baptism of Christ, the initiation and cause of the resurrection unto life when He comes again. Antony had failed to clarify the

---

[67]"Redemption," 138, 146.

[68]Ibid., 139.

[69]Ibid., 138.

[70]Florovsky, *Ways*, vol. 2, 210.

[71]"Redemption," 131–132.

[72]Florovsky published two homilies on the Ascension: the first is "Bogatstvo slavy: O Voznesenii Gospodnem," *Sergievskie listki / Feuillets de St-Serge* 9 (1930): 1–6, with an abridged English version as "Abundance of Glory (On the Ascension of our Lord)," *Journal of the Fellowship of St. Alban and St. Sergius* 9 (June 1930): 10–15; the second is "'And Ascended into Heaven'," *SVSQ* 2, no. 3 (Spring 1954): 23–28. Yet it is in his ecclesiological essays that one sees this theme most clearly developed.

distinction between *nature* and *will* in union with Christ. Florovsky, in response, follows Maximus the Confessor and Nicholas Cabasilas in the view that while Christ's death was the baptism of nature, resulting in resurrection for all, a freely willed response is needed for that resurrection to be blessed. Because baptism is a sacramental dying with Christ, it must be joined to a repentant dying to self, the path of the cross.[73]

The 1939 *In Ligno Crucis* essay published in 1976 under the title of "Redemption" also concludes with sacraments, this time the Eucharist. As Florovsky states, the sacramental significance of the Lord's death as the Passover of the New Testament is revealed at the Last Supper, which was itself a true sacrament: "an offering of the sacrifice of the Cross." "The Eucharist is the Last Supper itself, again and again enacted, but not repeated, for every new celebration does not only represent, but truly *is the same* 'Mystical Supper' which was celebrated for the first time by the High Priest Himself, 'in the night in which He was given up or rather gave Himself for the life of the world.'"[74] This "is the sacrament of the Crucifixion, the broken Body and the Blood outpoured," "the mysterious and sacramental 'conversion' of the flesh into the glorious spiritual food (μεταβολή)."[75] Florovsky draws especially on Chrysostom and Cabasilas in speaking of Christ's priestly ministry in the Eucharist. As he writes:

> The true Celebrant of each Liturgy is Our Lord Himself. . . . Christ is still acting as High Priest in His Church. The Mystery is all the same. The Sacrifice is one. The Table is one. The priest is the same. And not one Lamb is

[73]See the previous essay in the present volume. Florovsky would later describe this ascetic dimension in terms of i*mitatio Christi*. In "Redemption," an unpublished précis for his planned book on atonement written during the 1950s, he states: "Christ's life itself – the life of the Suffering Servant, in lowliness and humiliation – sets a new pattern and a new norm. It is the pattern of the New Kingdom. In this sense an *Imitatio Christi* is required and it has a redemptive significance. Actually, there is more than a pattern or just an example to be followed. Christians are summoned not only 'to follow' Christ, but to be *in Christo*. Gross misinterpretations of the mystery of Redemption were due, in the Ancient times and even more the present, to the disproportionate emphasis on the concept of pattern or example (e.g., Pelagius, Abelard). On the other hand, Christ was the Teacher and, indeed, the Only Teacher. The Evangelical pattern of life, as delineated in His Parables and in the Sermon on the Mount, belonged to the very structure of His redemptive ministry" (personal papers of Florovsky in my possession). Somewhat later, Florovsky remarked more simply: "*Imitatio Christi* is not just a figure of speech, and it is not a Western phrase. St Ignatius of Antioch regarded himself as a *mimetes Christou*, with special emphasis on the sharing of the Cross or the martyr's death": Gallaher, "Georges Florovsky on reading the Life of St Seraphim," 62–63. Florovsky's considerable balance here marks a notable contrast with Vladimir Lossky, *The Mystical Theology of the Eastern Church* (Crestwood, N.Y.: St. Vladimir's Seminary Press, 1998), 215.

[74]"Redemption," 157.

[75]Ibid., 134–5.

slain, or offered this day, and another of old; not one here, and another some-
where else. But *the same* always and everywhere ... The Eucharist is a sacrifice, not because Jesus is slain again, but because the same Body and the same
sacrificial Blood are actually here are the Altar, offered and presented.[76]

As Florovsky quotes Cabasilas: "In offering and sacrificing Himself once for all,
He did not cease from His priesthood, but He exercises this perpetual ministry
for us, in which He is our advocate with God for ever, for which reason it is said
of Him, Thou art a priest for ever."[77] In the Eucharist, Christ gives us an image
of the coming new creation, *and* builds up His Body, the Church, in history.

This sacramental conception of atonement is determinative for Florovsky's
later developed ecclesiology. Appealing to his favorite ecclesiological image
from Augustine's *Ennarationes in Psalmos,* Florovsky insisted repeatedly that
ecclesiology is the doctrine of the "Whole Christ"—*totus Christus, caput et corpus*—and, thus, an integral chapter of Christology.[78] Tempering recent attempts
to play Trinitarian or pneumatological conceptions of the Church against the
Christocentric, he was firm that the mystery of the Trinity "can only be apprehended through Christ,"[79] and that "the Spirit is the Spirit of Christ," whose
work is to unite us to Christ: "the Pentecost is the mystery of the Crucified
Lord."[80]

Florovsky thus speaks of the Church in Chalcedonian terms—again, positively, dynamically interpreted. "The crucial point," he says, is "the character of
Christ's 'human nature,' his own and yet universal." Yet "the concept of Incarnation, taken by itself and not expanded sufficiently to include the life and work
of Christ up to their climax on the Cross and in the glory of the Resurrection,
does not provide a sufficient ground or basis for ecclesiology. Nor would it
be sufficient to analyze the mystery of the Incarnation exclusively in terms of
'nature.'" Rather, "the doctrine of the Church can be developed only within the
comprehensive scheme of the divine *oikonomia* of salvation."[81] That is to say:

---

[76]Ibid., 157.

[77]Ibid., 158.

[78]Cf. Augustine, *Enarrationes in Psalmos* 58.1.2 (PL 36:693).

[79]Florovsky, "Patristic Theology and the Ethos of the Orthodox Church," *Aspects of Church
History,* 24.

[80]Gallaher, "Georges Florovsky on reading the Life of St Seraphim," 62; for discussion, see
Baker, "The Eternal 'Spirit of the Son'," 164n.

[81]Florovsky, "Christ and His Church: Suggestions and Comments," in *L'Église et les Églises,
1054–1954, neuf siècles de douloureuse séparation entre l'Orient et l'Occident, études travaux sur l'unité
chrétienne offerts à Dom Lambert Beauduin 2,* Collection Irénikon (Chevtogne: Editions de Cheve-
togne, 1955), 159–70, at 167.

the Church is not only the sacrament of Christ's person, but also the recapitulation of all His *work*.

The key here is in the sacraments.[82] As Florovsky cites Nicholas Cabasilas: "the sacraments signify and are the Church."[83] And "the whole celebration of the Mystery is one image of the whole economy of our Lord,"[84] "a comprehensive image of Christ's redemptive *oikonomia*."[85] Hence, as Cabasilas says, in a phrase that encapsulates the heart of Florovsky's own mysteriology: "introduction to the mysteries is as to a kind of 'body of history.'"[86] It is thus that, constituted in the sacraments, the Church is a "summary" of Christ's redeeming work.[87] Her form is the form of redemption, according to the Chalcedonian pattern. As Florovsky writes:

> The "form of the servant" is obvious in the Church. But faith discerns under this "form," or rather within it, "the new creation" and the abiding presence of Christ, through the Spirit. The life of Christians "is hid with Christ in God" (Col 3:3). The "two lives" are united and interrelated in the identity of subject: unconfusedly, unchangeably, indivisibly, inseparably. There is but one Church, "visible" and "invisible" at once, humiliated and glorious at once. The human condition is not abrogated by divine grace but only redeemed and transfigured.[88]

[82]Here Florovsky confesses his debt to the *Mysterientheologie* of Dom Odo Casel and to Maurice de la Taille's 1921 work on the Eucharist, *Mysterium Fidei*; see Florovsky, "Redemption," 301n100 and 308n154. There is some indication that it may have been his reading of these two Roman Catholic scholars that compelled Florovsky to pay close attention to the sacramental theology of Nicholas Cabasilas, who together with Chrysostom would form the most important Greek patristic source for his thinking on the sacraments. Later, while dean of St Vladimir's Seminary, Florovsky taught a seminar entitled "The Doctrine of Atonement" in which de la Taille's study was assigned reading (syllabus found in personal papers of Florovsky, in my possession). Florovsky's later reading of Cabasilas was also impacted by the work of Myrrha Lot-Borodine; his review of her work appears in *GOTR* 4, no. 2 (Winter 1958–1959): 191–194.

[83]Florovsky, "The Eucharist and Catholicity" [1929], in *Ecumenism I: A Doctrinal Approach* (vol. 13 of *Collected works of Georges Florovsky*; ed. Richard Haugh; Vaduz, Liechtenstein: Büchervertriebsanstalt, 1989), 54. An unfinished chapter on the Eucharist and the Church, entitled "The Ultimate Mystery," is included amongst Florovsky's additions to *In Ligno Crucis* from the 1950s. Here again, as in his earlier treatments of the sacraments and ecclesiology, the key sources are Chrysostom, Nicholas Cabasilas, and Augustine (personal papers of Florovsky in my possession, given to me by Andrew Blane).

[84]"Redemption," 158.

[85]Florovsky, "Patristic Theology and the Ethos of the Orthodox Church," 24.

[86]Florovsky, "The Eucharist and Catholicity," 5.

[87]Florovsky, "Christ and His Church: Suggestions and Comments," 167.

[88]Florovsky, "Togetherness in Christ," in *The Unity We Seek* (ed. William S. Morris; Oxford: Oxford University Press, 1963), 17–27, at 19–20.

Atonement and the *Telos* of Creation

Florovsky was assuredly not one of those who speak of *theosis,* communion, or the "sacramentality of creation" without mentioning the need for objective redemption from sin and death. Yet, he stressed, "'soteriology itself culminates in the concept of 'New Creation.'"[89] This consideration brings us to the last major point of Florovsky's thinking on atonement: the question of the "ultimate motive" of the incarnation, and its relationship to the overarching design of creation.

Would God have become man even if man had not fallen? Florovsky treats this question briefly in his 1951 essay "The Lamb of God" and again in his 1957 article, "*Cur Deus Homo?* The Motive of the Incarnation," the latter of which was, as noted above, originally intended as a chapter of the book on atonement on which he had begun to work again in the 1950s.[90] As usual, he stresses the need to stay close to the actual pattern of accomplished historical events:

> We may not deal with abstract possibilities, actually unrealized and frustrated, nor build the doctrinal synthesis on the analysis of probabilities . . . we have to deal with the *fact* of the Incarnation, and not with its idea . . . we know the Incarnate Lord *only* as our *Saviour* . . . the Crucified and Risen One. The Son of God "came down into a *fallen* world, to seek and bring back the *lost* sheep."[91]

Nevertheless, he argues, "There are certain theological reasons for regarding the Incarnation as an integral part of the original plan of Creation . . . an organic consummation of the primordial creative purpose of God . . . not . . . essentially dependent on the Fall, i.e. upon the disruption of this purpose by the revolt and depravation of the creature."[92]

With a deliberate echo of Anselm in its title, Florovsky's "*Cur Deus Homo*"[93] cautiously advances this argument with reference to such medieval schoolmen as

---

[89]Florovsky, "Patristic Theology and the Ethos of the Orthodox Church," 25.

[90]"The Lamb of God," *Scottish Journal of Theology* 4, no. 1 (1951): 13–28; "*Cur Deus Homo?* The Motive of the Incarnation," in *Creation and Redemption,* 163–70.

[91]Florovsky, "The Lamb of God," 21.

[92]Florovsky, "The Lamb of God," 20–21.

[93]As Jaroslav Pelikan has noted, here Florovsky addresses a problem that "has been fundamental to the Augustinian heritage of Western theology: how to affirm simultaneously the goodness of the Creation and the necessity of the Incarnation": see "Puti Russkogo Bogoslova: When Orthodoxy Comes West," in *The Heritage of the Early Church: Essays in Honor of Georges Vasilievich Florovsky* (eds. David Nieman and Margaret Schatkin; Rome: Pontifical Oriental Institute, 1973), 11–16, at 12.

Rupert of Deutz, Alexander of Hales, Albertus Magnus, Aquinas, Bonaventure, and Duns Scotus. The essay is a model of the dialogue with Latin scholasticism on a patristic basis called for in the conclusion to *Ways of Russian Theology*.[94] Florovsky finds in Maximus the Confessor support for the Scotist view of the Incarnation as the first object of God's creative will, for which all things were created—a matter of absolute predestination, independent of man's fall. This, he notes, is but a *theologoumenon*, but one that fits well within the general scheme of patristic doctrine. He concludes: "An adequate answer to the question of the 'motive' of the Incarnation can only be given in the context of the general doctrine of Creation."[95]

Conclusion

How successful is Florovsky's soteriological synthesis? The comprehensive force of Florovsky's vision is obvious, and it seems to me that Florovsky has placed the accent in all the right places: the centrality of singular historical events in redemption, the unity of Christ's person and work, the objective and universal redeeming character of Christ's death on the Cross, atonement as liturgy and sacrament giving shape to the Church and her mission, atonement as the fulfillment of Creation.

Yet we must mark two serious lacunae. First, the *Father*. "God so loved the world that he gave his only begotten Son" (John 3:16). "God was in Christ, reconciling the world to Himself" (2 Cor 5:19). God "made him sin who knew no sin" (2 Cor 5:21). Florovsky makes almost no mention of the work of the Father as initiator of atonement—a motif we find in St Philaret and, more problematically, Bulgakov. Yet it is a crucial biblical theme.

[94]Cf. Ways, vol. 2, 294–308. The degree to which Florovsky's critique of scholasticism in *Ways of Russian Theology* was really a critique of the second-hand Baroque *neo*-scholasticism of the manualist tradition has been missed by many readers. As Florovsky described the problem in a later essay: "Theological habits and schemes were borrowed from the West, rather eclectically, both from the late Roman scholasticism of Post-Tridentine times and from the various theologies of the Reformation." In Florovsky, "Patristic Theology and the Ethos of the Orthodox Church," 20.

[95]"Cur Deus Homo," 170. As George Williams notes, Florovsky's interest in the question of "the predestination of the Redeemer" was provoked by the work of the Roman Catholic theologian Joseph Pohle, *Soteriology: A Dogmatic Treatise on Redemption* (London, 1947), 24–34: George H. Williams, "Georges Vasilevich Florovsky: His American Career (1948–1965)," 71. On Maximus, see further: Florovsky, "Maximos und der Origenismus," *Diskussionsbeiträge zum XI. Internationalen Byzantisten-Kongress München 1958* (Munich: C.H. Beck, 1961), 38–40 (comments by Florovsky in English); and Florovsky, "The Christological Dogma and its Terminology," in *Christ in East and West* (ed. Paul Fries and Tiran Nersoyan; Macon, Ga.: Mercer University Press, 1987), 45–47, at 46.

Somewhat related to this is the issue of law and substitution. "For what the law could not do, in that it was weak through the flesh, God sending his own Son in the likeness of sinful flesh, and for sin, condemned sin in the flesh; that the righteousness of the law might be fulfilled in us, who walk not after the flesh, but after the Spirit" (Rom 8:3–4). Recalling that Theophan of Poltava had attacked Antony Khrapovitsky for denying substitutionary atonement, it is curious to find that a later version of Florovsky's atonement essay, the 1953 "On the Tree of the Cross," informs its readers that Theophan had praised "the original manuscript" as "the first modern Russian theological work" which presented the doctrine of atonement "in a strict Orthodox manner."[96] This is curious, because Florovsky, almost as much as Antony, downplays—almost dismisses—the substitutionary and legal language of Scripture, calling it "colorless anthropomorphism."[97]

Such dismissal, however, threatens to undermine precisely that *objectivity* of Christ's atoning work and the "metaphysical realism" of the Fathers that Florovsky so seeks to protect. One may dare to say that the Greek Fathers took such Scriptural language more seriously. St Athanasius, for instance, tells us that Christ died as a "substitute" (ἀντίψυχον)[98], "in the stead of all" (ἀντὶ πάντων),[99] accomplishing not only His own death, but "the death of men"; becoming "a curse" and paying in our stead the debt exacted by the law.[100] "Formerly the world, as guilty, was under the judgment from the law," says Athanasius, "but now the Word has taken on the judgment, and having suffered in the body for all, has bestowed salvation on all."[101] Similar language can be found in the Cappadocians and in St Cyril of Alexandria.

[96]Florovsky, "On the Tree of the Cross," *SVSQ* 3–4 (Spring–Summer 1953): 11. Ironically, Khrapovitsky also gave the highest accolades to Florovsky: "Your special merit is your strict loyalty to the teaching of the Orthodox Church and Faith, and yet without any detriment to the historic impartiality, as you rigidly and faithfully distinguish the Tradition of the Church from all alien accretions": quoted in Alexander Schmemann, "Roll of Honour," *SVSQ* 2, no. 1 (Fall 1953), 5–11, at 7. A letter from Khrapovitsky to Florovsky dating from the late 1920s rests in the library of St Vladimir's Seminary (Florovsky Papers, Box 1, B, 1).

[97]Florovsky, "Redemption," 101; see also 102–103. This treatment stands in tension with the more positive theological interpretation of biblical anthropomorphism characteristic of Florovsky's essays on Scripture.

[98]Athanasius, *De Incarnatione*, 9.2, 37.7 in SC 199 (ed. Charles Kannengiesser; 2000), 294–96, 398.

[99]Athanasius, *De Incarnatione*, 9.1, 10.1–2, 20.2 (SC 199, 294, 298–300, 336–38).

[100]Athanasius, *De Incarnatione*, 22.3, 25.2, 6.2–3, 9.4, 20.5 (SC 199, 346, 354–56, 282–84, 296–98, 338).

[101]Athanasius, *Contra Arianos* 1.60 in, *Athanasius Werke* 1.1.2 (ed. Karin Metzler and Kyriakos Savvidis; Berlin: Walter de Gruyter, 1998), 171. Related to this matter also is Florovsky's rather

More remarkable, perhaps, is the example of St Nicholas Cabasilas. In Book Four of his *The Life in Christ*—precisely where Florovsky so relies on him in his treatment of the Eucharist—Nicholas makes use of terminology which some scholars have suggested may be compared with that of Anselm—although the first Greek translation of Anselm's *Cur Deus Homo* would seem to postdate Cabasilas—and Cabasilas' work is marked by the very significant difference of situating such atonement discourse in a mysteriological context, which Anselm's most notably does not do. In the Eucharist, says Cabasilas, we receive that body in which Christ rendered honor (τιμήν) to the Father by His life, and by His death and ascension to the Father's glory made satisfaction (ἀπολογήσασθαι) for the debt of honor we owed (ὀφειλόμεθα τιμήν) by reason of our sins.[102] Again, while Florovsky states that "the Cross is not a symbol of Justice, but the symbol of Love Divine,"[103] Nicholas' contemporary St Gregory Palamas speaks of the Cross and the descent into Hades as an act of "justice" without which, he says, "God does not act."[104] In all these Fathers, what is striking is how the language of substitution is consistently held together with that of union, divine victory, and *theosis*, the conceptuality of law together with that of nature.

Florovsky described his projected neo-patristic synthesis as an "ecumenical synthesis," in which divided lines of Christian thought were to be reintegrated on a patristic basis. In his essay on Jeremiah II and the Lutheran divines, he stated that Philip Melanchthon's "attempt to interpret the message of the Reformation in the wider context of an ecumenical tradition embracing the East and the West should be repeated," with "all controversial points, dividing the East from the non-Roman West . . . analyzed again in the larger perspective of Patristic tradition."[105] Neither the Reformers' nor Anselm's theories, of course, can be identified with the atonement theology of such Fathers as Athanasius

---

one-sided emphasis on the prelapsarian character of the humanity assumed by the *Logos*: on this, see the discussion in Matthew Baker, "The Place of St. Irenaeus of Lyons in Historical and Dogmatic Theology according to Thomas F. Torrance," *Participatio: The Journal of the T.F Torrance Theological Fellowship* 2 (2010): 5–43, esp. 26–27; also, John Meyendorff, "Christ's Humanity: The Paschal Mystery," *SVTQ* 31 (1987): 5–40.

[102]Nicholas Cabasilas, *On the Life in Christ*, 4.4 in SC 355 (ed. Marie-Hélène Congourdeau; 1989), 264–66; see also 4.5 (SC 355, 266).

[103]Florovsky, "Redemption," 103.

[104]Homily 16 on Great and Holy Saturday (PG 151:189–220); Christopher Veniamin, trans., *Saint Gregory Palamas: The Homilies* (South Canaan, Pa.: Mount Thabor Publishing, 2009).

[105]"An Early Ecumenical Correspondence (Patriarch Jeremiah II and the Lutheran Divines)," in *Christianity and Culture*, 155; see also Florovsky, "The Greek Version of the Augsburg Confession," ibid., 157–160.

or Cabasilas. Yet Cabasilas shows us, at least, the possibility that Anselm can be interpreted, with charity, similarly in a wider perspective.[106]

Like Khrapovitsky, Florovsky's atonement essays of the 1930s were written still under the influence of the moral expiation theory of Kazan Academy professor Victor Ivanovich Nesmelov (1863–1937), to the 1971 re-edition of whose book the *Science of Man* he had written a foreword.[107] However, a number of dated volumes relating to Anselm and atonement in Florovsky's personal library housed at St Vladimir's Seminary indicate that he was revisiting the topic of atonement in the 1950s, during which time he had again returned to working on his projected book on atonement. Florovsky's repeated positive invocation of the mottos *fides quaerens intellectum* and *credo ut intelligam* in his essays of this period suggest possibly some greater consideration of Anselm in general.[108] In his 1956 essay on eschatology in the patristic age, Florovsky does not hesitate to cite positively Thomas Cranmer's eucharistic canon from the *Book of Common Prayer*, describing the sacrifice of the Cross as "a full, perfect, and sufficient sacrifice, oblation and satisfaction."[109]

Florovsky's early ambivalence regarding the so-called "substitutionary" character of atonement is not unique, but representative of much of Orthodox theology of the last century.[110] We have been too imprisoned in the simplistic schema popularized by the Swedish Lutheran Gustaf Aulen's 1931 study, *Christus Victor*, between a Greek patristic and Lutheran "dramatic" theory and a Latin and Reformed "satisfaction" theory. Too often, understanding of

[106] As has recently been attempted by David Hart, "A Gift Exceeding Every Debt: An Eastern Orthodox Appreciation of Anselm's *Cur Deus Homo*," *Pro Ecclesia* 7, no. 3 (1998): 333–348. See also: Oliver Herbel, "Anselm the Neo-Nestorian? Responding to the Accusation in Light of *On the Incarnation of the Word*," *SVTQ* 52, no. 2 (2008): 173–97. Richard Swinburne, *Responsibility and Atonement* (Oxford: Oxford University Press, 1989), is critical of legal metaphors but retrieves the notion of debt-payment as understood within the context of sacrifice.

[107] *Nauka o cheloveke* (Farnborough, Hampshire, UK: Gregg, 1971). As Nikolay Gavriushin has commented in a severely critical essay, "while Florovsky intends initially to provide a radical critique of the doctrine of redemption developed by Metropolitan Anthony Khrapovitsky, Florovsky himself basically goes down the same path ... Anthony grew up in conversations with Nesmelov": N. Gavriushin, " '... Chtoby istoshchilos' uporstvo razdora.' Shtrikhi k portretu G.V. Florovskogo," *Simvol* 47 (2004): 201–238.

[108] For references and discussion, see Matthew Baker, " 'Theology Reasons' – in History: Neo-patristic Synthesis and the Renewal of Theological Rationality," in Θεολογία 81, no. 4 (2010): 81–118, at 98–99 and 112nn89 and 112.

[109] Florovsky, "The Patristic Age and Eschatology," *Aspects of Church History*, 65.

[110] A great exception would appear to be Fr Dumitru Staniloae, who offers a balanced integration of substitutionary, legal, and cultic dimensions of the work of Christ: see *The Person of Jesus Christ as God and Savior* (The Experience of God: Orthodox Dogmatic Theology 3; Brookline, Mass.: Holy Cross Orthodox Press, 2011).

traditional atonement language has been obscured by confessional polemics and by the influence of modern existentialism, with its antinomian tendencies. As one Jesuit commentator, Bernard Schultze, noted in his 1946 review of modern Russian treatments of soteriology:

> Legalism has truly become for many theologians . . . a kind of bogeyman that scares away the free use of the human intellectual faculties. But it would be appropriate to refer the legal concept to an unbiased testing and to analyze this idea philosophically, before running away frightened. There is a lack of this in all these works by Eastern theologians.[111]

A more honest study of the language of substitution, debt-satisfaction, ransom, and law in general within patristic literature is thus in order for Orthodox theology today. The language of substitution and debt as is found in Scripture and the Fathers must be interpreted and rightly appropriated, not dismissed. If this proves repellent to us, we only show ourselves to be, not the children of the Fathers, but of that figure whose influence Florovsky critiqued in Antony Khrapovitsky: Immanuel Kant, who in his *Religion within the Limits of Reason Alone* denied that any person can pay another's debt of sin. With all the talk about overcoming Western individualism in favor of a "relational ontology," many modern Orthodox theologians, in their rejection of vicarious atonement and their inability to think about ontology and law together, are still, like their Western cousins, children of the Enlightenment.[112]

It is here, however, that, in its broadest and most fundamental concerns, Florovsky's great and abiding contribution is to be found. Florovsky's theology of history, his affirmation of the permanent and effective power of singular *events*, entails a profound critique of Enlightenment and historicist conceptions of time and the Pelagian moralism which must accompany any theology which adopts these. This includes the most recent version of such Pelagian moralism: the confusion of redemption with the struggle for social justice. Benedict XVI, long before becoming pope of Rome, named the central crisis of our time as the "Heideggerian problematic" of "understanding the mediation of history in the realm of ontology."[113] Florovsky's interpretation of salvation as dependent upon

---

[111]Bernard Schultze, "La nuova soteriologia russa," *OCP* 12 (1946), at 143–44, at 154.

[112]For a remarkable attempt to integrate the conceptualities of law, credit, and debt into a creative adaptation of Zizioulas's relational ontology, and with an Irenaeus-inspired account of divine economy, see Douglas Knight, *The Eschatological Economy: Time and the Hospitality of God* (Grand Rapids, Mich.: Eerdmans, 2006).

[113]Joseph Ratzinger, *Principles of Catholic Theology: Building Stones for a Fundamental Theology* (trans. Mary Frances McCarthy; San Francisco: Ignatius Press, 1987), 160.

events at once historically contingent and eschatologically decisive allows him to face modern philosophical hermeneutics head-on, with the confidence that the equally contingent character of interpretation that marks all our knowledge of these saving events in no way empties the realism and universality of their claim. This is because such interpretations are grounded in the ecclesial body of the incarnate Lord of history. In the Church, the originating events of salvation—the incarnation, Cross, and resurrection—are made permanently present and have their effective history through the sacraments.

In spite of all the postmodern critique of Enlightenment universalism in the recognition of the historical constitution of knowledge, the same anti-historical *Aufklärung* tendency Florovsky criticized—the inability to apprehend specific historically contingent events as absolute truth, permanently and universally effective upon all—remains at work in the Liberal theology of today as it increasingly engages in inter-religious dialogue with non-Christian religions. This is expressed as an acute discomfort with the proclamation that Jesus Christ is the one Saviour of the world—not simply *a* way, but *the* way; not simply for Christians, but for all mankind. In the face of this challenge, Florovsky's theology reasserts with relentless force, profundity and startling consistency the "scandal of particularity" upon which the entire Gospel stands: that "when the fullness of the time had come, God sent forth His Son, born*[a]* of a woman, born under the law, to redeem those who were under the law, that we might receive the adoption as sons" (Gal 4:4–5).

PART II

GEORGES FLOROVSKY ON ATONEMENT

✠

Introduction

Matthew Baker and Seraphim Danckaert

B ELOW ARE FOUR WRITINGS by Fr Georges Florovsky. Two have never been published before, one has only appeared in Swedish in a hard-to-find academic journal, and the last is a sermon, originally published in a collection now out of print. Taken together, these four items are far more suggestive than systematic, but they provide a concise and insightful discussion of the major issues.

The first three writings represent different stages of Florovsky's decades-long attempt to write a substantial book on the patristic or Orthodox understanding of redemption. We have not made an attempt to reproduce all of the various manuscripts—there are many—or to provide a complete history of Florovsky's revisions and attempted publications. Rather, we have chosen a few items that show two things: first, his abiding interest in the topic, and, second, his consistent approach. All of these writings place the atoning sacrifice of Christ and His redemptive work in the largest possible context, drawing an arc across the entire divine economy of salvation, including creation, incarnation, ministry, death on the Cross, descent into hell, resurrection, ascension, and, quite importantly, the ascended Jesus's continued redeeming presence in the Church as "both Sacrifice and Priest." All of these writings consider Christology itself as the proper context for the discussion, and they also emphasize the liturgical, sacramental, and even ascetical dimensions of atonement and redemption.

Yet each item brings forth a particular melody or motif in a larger symphony. We will highlight unique elements below as well as explain the provenance of the unpublished material.

In Ligno Crucis: **Ad Lectorem**

Florovsky wrote this unpublished work in France in 1939. It was to serve as the preface to a short book, eighty-one pages in typescript, based on his lectures examining the patristic doctrine of atonement. James Clarke and Co Ltd, London had agreed to publish the work. Perhaps because of the war, it never appeared. Had it been printed, it would have represented Florovsky's very first published use of "neo-patristic synthesis," that famous phrase that continues to define his legacy.

Florovsky further revised the complete text in 1948, the year he emigrated to America,[1] and continued to rework and expand the book, publishing excerpts in the late 1940s and early 1950s in article form under the titles "The Lamb of God" and "On the Tree of the Cross."[2] Further new additions were made in the same decade, a portion of which became the brief essay "*Cur Deus Homo?* The Motive of the Incarnation."[3] Yet the intended book never appeared.

Finally, in 1976 a version nearly identical to the 1939 and 1948 manuscripts appeared under the title of "Redemption" in volume 3 of Florovsky's *Collected Works*. None of the expanded material from the 1950s was included, although "*Cur Deus Homo*" was published separately in the same volume. The decision to publish "Redemption" in its earlier form is understandable. Much of Florovsky's additional material is in rough condition, and there are multiple versions in which Florovsky proposes different ways of organizing the expanded book. Taken by itself, however, "Redemption" does somewhat obscure Florovsky's larger vision, particularly as that vision evolved over decades of reflection. For example, one gets a very different sense of Florovsky's approach if one reads "Redemption" alongside "*Cur Deus Homo*," as Florovsky suggested is necessary. Reading the two together as part of a larger work provides more attention to the soteriological implications of the doctrine of creation, a deeper engagement with the medieval schoolmen, more assessment of modern Western theologies, and an even greater role for St Maximus the Confessor—all characteristics emphasized in the "Précis" published below as well.

[1]We have printed the 1948 preface, which is slightly revised, as contained in Andrew Blane's collection of Florovsky's personal papers, which is currently in the possession of Katherine Baker. One can also find the manuscripts in the Princeton archive. For the 1939 unrevised typescript see Princeton CO586 Box 2, folder 1, and for the 1948 revised typescript see Princeton CO586, Box 3, folder 4.

[2]Georges Florovsky, "The Lamb of God," in *Lovet være Du Jesus Krist. Inkarnationen. Seks Forelæsninger* (ed. L. Berner-Schilden-Holsten; Bringstrup: Theologisk oratoriums forlag, 1949): 66–83; repr. in *Scottish Journal of Theology* 4, no. 1 (1951): 13–28. Idem., "On the Tree of the Cross," *SVSQ* 1 (1953): 11–34.

[3]"Cur Deus Homo? The Motive of the Incarnation," in Εὐχαριστήριον, τιμητικὸς τόμος ἐπὶ τῇ 45ἐτηρίδι τῆς ἐπιστημονικῆς δράσεως καὶ τῇ 35ἐτηρίδι τακτικῆς καθηγεσίας Ἀμίλκα Σ. Ἀλιβιζάτου [*Eucharisterion, Festschrift for the 45th Anniversary as a Scholar of Prof. Hamilcar Alivisatos*] (Athens: n.p., 1957), 70–79; repr. in Florovsky, *Creation and Redemption* (vol. 3 of *Collected works of Georges Florovsky*; Belmont, MA: Nordland, 1976), 163–170, 310–314.

[4]Florovsky's lectures were published in 1987 in the Collected Works of Georges Florovsky as vol. 10, *Byzantine Ascetic and Spiritual Fathers* (Vaduz, Liechtenstein: Buchvertriebsanstalt, 1987). The Russian original has yet to be published.

At any rate, the main oversight of "Redemption" as published in 1976 is that it fails to include the original preface. Perhaps there was confusion over the many manuscripts, but the lack of inclusion may also have been a deliberate choice on the part of the editor. Florovsky's preface is a little unusual—at least at first glance. It makes a few points about the topic it purports to introduce, but a large section pursues what appears to be a tangent: "Christian Hellenism." Upon closer examination, however, one can see the argument unfold. Christian Hellenism, in Florovsky's conception, is the *intellectual tradition* of the Church Fathers, both East and West. He is, therefore, making a plea for the inclusion of a rigorous metaphysics in Christian doctrine—a "baptized" metaphysics grounded in historical events and unique to the Church Fathers. Without awareness of the Church's intellectual tradition—without a theology attuned to the epistemological, metaphysical, and anthropological precepts that cohere in the doctrinal system of the ecumenical teachers of the Church—most discussions of "atonement" devolve into moralism or psychology. A very careful reader might discern this thesis within the pages of "Redemption" itself, but it certainly helps to have some explicit direction in the preface. It also helps to clarify a broader question: why Florovsky placed such an emphasis on the Hellenic character of Christian theology in general. In fact, this preface contains Florovsky's clearest and most succinct exposition of what is really behind his emphasis on Christian Hellenism: "Hellenism means philosophy," he writes, a kind of "Christian philosophy" found in the Fathers that is "a new philosophical synthesis on the basis of the Revelation."

Certain verbal cues in the preface suggest there is another issue at play. Behind the talk of Hellenism and the Reformation's repudiation of philosophy itself—a narrative sketched already in the 1930 essay "The Crisis of German Idealism"—Florovsky has in mind the dialectical theology of Emil Brunner, and perhaps also the early Karl Barth. Florovsky's letters to Barth's friend Fritz Lieb indicate that Florovsky thought of his own work on atonement in critical relation to that of Brunner and was eager to hear Barth's opinion on this. In a 1928 review of Brunner's book *The Mediator*, Florovsky had criticized Brunner for continuing the anti-Hellenism of the nineteenth-century Liberal Protestant theologians Ritschl and Harnack, even while attacking Liberal theology. Florovsky's argument here in his preface has a sharp irony: while even the hypostatic union seems "too metaphysical" to this form of Protestant theology, the rejection of the Christian philosophy of the Fathers results in *greater* abstraction in the doctrine of atonement, "much more abstract than the patristic metaphysics."

It is these connections and debates, never fully spelled out, that explain the attention given to Christian Hellenism in the preface.

In Ligno Crucis (A Summary from Sweden)

In the fall of 1946, Florovsky lectured on the doctrine of atonement at Lund University and Aarhus University, in Sweden and Demark respectively. At that time Lund was a place of burgeoning interest in patristic theology among Lutheran scholars, hosting a succession of luminaries, which included Gustaf Aulén (1879–1978), Anders Nygren (1890–1978) and, soon after, Gustaf Wingren (1910–2000).

Florovsky took an interest in Swedish theology as early as 1931–1933, when he made a point to frame his lectures on ascetic theology at St Serge in terms of a refutation of Anders Nygren's 1930 book *Agape and Eros*.[4] In his letters to Fritz Lieb, Florovsky indicates that he was engaged in a deep study of Luther and of the Protestant theology of the nineteenth century. In September 1937, Florovsky was honored with a doctorate of divinity from the University of St Andrews together with Gustav Aulén and Karl Barth. Aulén's influential 1931 book, *Christus Victor*, had stressed a return to what Aulén understood as the Greek patristic doctrine of atonement. In Aulén's reading, the Fathers understood atonement as divine victory over death and a ransoming of mankind from Hades. Aulén argued that this patristic view had been revived in the thought of Luther, as counterposed to the "Latin" and Reformed doctrine of atonement as satisfaction, and equally against the moral exemplarist or subjective view characteristic of Abelard and of nineteenth-century Liberal Protestant theology. Although Florovsky's theology of atonement differs from that of Aulén on account of Florovsky's dyothelite stress on the full human willing agency of Christ, his lectures share with Aulén an unmistakable accent upon divine victory.

The work published below is the first-ever English translation of an article that originally appeared in Swedish in the scholarly journal of Lund's Faculty of Theology. Florovsky had given a written copy of his lectures—quite similar to the 1939 manuscript described above—to a professor at Lund, Bengt Strömberg, who turned the full manuscript into a concise article in Swedish of less than 4,500 words. The summary lacks the copious references and lengthy quotes from the Church Fathers found in the full version, but the summary's concision makes it very easy to follow the actual argument, even if in truncated form. As such, it presents the reader with a very brief overview of Florovsky's approach to the doctrine of atonement, one that is broadly representative of all of his various attempts to discuss the topic. It is clear that Florovsky found serious fault with any "theory" of atonement that places too much emphasis on substitution, satisfaction, and even sacrifice, if sacrifice is understood as penal instead of leading to a glorious victory that opens up a new eucharistic reality within the Church.

In addition to its value as a summary, the Swedish article represents the very first published use of what would become Florovsky's most famous phrase: "neo-patristic synthesis."

Redemption (A Précis of a Planned Book)

This précis comes from a typescript found in Andrew Blane's personal collection of Florovsky's papers, now in the care of Katherine Baker. The manuscript is a proposal that Florovsky sent to a publisher. It is quite interesting and important for understanding his thoughts on the matter as they developed over time.

The Stumbling-Block

Florovsky took up the theme of the Cross and the Suffering Servant in a number of sermons. "The Stumbing-Block" is an example of Florovsky's homiletic approach to these issues, originally published in 1963 as the only Orthodox contribution to a volume entitled *Preaching the Passion: Twenty-Four Outstanding Sermons for the Lenten Season.* Ending the present volume with a sermon was no casual choice. In many places, Florovsky emphasized that patristic theology is inherently exegetical and kerygmatic. The sermon is the true venue for theology. In addition, the sermon includes a brief reflection on the redemptive significance of the continuing priesthood of the ascended Jesus, bringing us back to the issues we raised in our preface.

In Ligno Crucis:
The Patristic Doctrine of the Atonement

by the Very Reverend George Florovsky, D.D.

"*Morte occisus, mortem occidit.*"—St Augustine

1948

In Memoriam

Walter Howard Frere

C.R.

Formerly Bishop of Truro,

First President of the Anglo-Russian Fellowship

of St Alban and St Sergius

✠

"Ad Lectorem"
Georges Florovsky

T HIS SMALL BOOK IS NOT A HISTORICAL STUDY, nor is it to be regarded as a chapter in a dogmatic system. My purpose is much more limited. It is an attempt to bring forward certain features of the patristic teaching, almost forgotten or neglected by the modern theologians, even in the churches of the catholic tradition, and to prove that just by this return to the Fathers one may regain a solid basis for theological research. This essay is but a pointer toward what one may describe as a *neo-patristic synthesis*. Dr G. L. Prestige's recent book, *God in Patristic Thought*, has clearly shown how much a modern theologian can profit by an unprejudiced and open-minded reading of the patristic writings. "*Inexhaustum est penum theologiae patrum*," said one of the seventeenth-century theologians.[1]

In modern times, patristic writings have been, and are still, usually read rather as merely historical documents. For their inspiration, modern theologians usually look elsewhere. They have much more concern with what is taken to be the "modern mind" than with what is referred to as the "venerable tradition" of the Church. But the real trouble about this so-called "modern mind" is that one cannot very easily discover what it really is. It was recently suggested that possibly the "modern man" has not yet made up his mind, and that perhaps it is preferable to speak rather only of the "modern temper" or "modern mood." One may speak rather of a modern chaos than of any settled mind today. In any case it would be very precarious to allow our theological interpretation to depend so much upon the "temper" of any particular age, upon all these changes and chances of this fleeting world. One has to rely, not upon the mind of any age, but solely upon the *mind of the Church*. The whole authority of the Fathers rests just upon the fact that they were the Doctors *of the Church*. It is true, however, that the main objection to the pattern authority of the Fathers is just that they too were limited by their own age. In a way that is indeed true, they were

---

[1]See my paper, Georges Florovsky, "Patristics and Modern Theology," *Procès-verbaux du Premier Congrès de Théologie orthodoxe à Athènes* (ed. Hamilcar Alivisatos,; Athens, 1939), 238–42; repr. in *The Christian East* 18, no. 1–2 (January–June 1936), 30–34.

interpreting the New Testament message in Greek categories, and the influence of Hellenistic philosophy on their conceptions must not be overlooked. Yet the real question is whether we can regard this "Hellenistic phase" of Christian theology merely as a historic accident, and whether we can ever get away from these Greek categories. Strangely enough, Harnack's thesis that patristic doctrine was simply an "acute Hellenization" of primitive Christianity still keeps its strong grip upon catholic-minded scholars. There are so many who would shrink from any suggestions that we are not Hellenized enough and that the only remedy for the modern chaos in theology is just this move back to the Greek tradition.

The problem is obviously too vast to be dealt with properly in a brief forward to an occasional essay. But we can hardly escape raising it here. Christian Hellenism is much wider than one is prepared to realize. St Augustine and even St Jerome were no less Hellenistic than St Gregory of Nyssa and St Chrysostom. And St Augustine introduced Neo-Platonism into Western theology. Pseudo-Dionysius was influential in the West no less than in the East, from Hilduin up to Nicholas of Cusa. And St John of Damascus was an authority both for the Byzantine Middle Ages and for Peter Lombard and Thomas Aquinas. Thomism itself is Hellenistic. In England, the Caroline divines were obviously Hellenistic in tendency. And one of the greatest contributions of the Tractarian movement was just this move back to the Greek Fathers. Christian Hellenism was never a peculiarly Eastern phenomenon.

The Fathers were teachers of the Church Universal, not just of the Eastern Church. Hellenism is the common background and the basis of the whole Christian civilization. It is simply incorporated into our Christian existence. One cannot easily undo the whole of history once it has been lived. Nor is there any reason to long for that. Somebody has wittily remarked that in a way the battle of Marathon belonged to English history no less than the battle of Hastings. With much more justification we can insist that the ecumenical councils and Greek patristics do belong to our own history, whatever our local allegiance may be. Hellenism was, of course, ambiguous and double-faced. And some of the Hellenistic revivals in the history of European thought have obviously been rather pagan revivals. It is enough to mention Goethe or Nietzsche. But we have not to overlook the existence of another Hellenism.

Hellenism itself was dissected with the sword of Christian revelation, and was polarized. So too was Judaism. May I suggest a pair of symbols to illustrate this polarity: the Acropolis and St Sophia. Both are truly Hellenistic. And yet St Sophia is in very truth a Christian temple. One has to go back not to Plato or Aristotle, but to the Greek Fathers, who were by no means simply Christian

Platonists or Aristotelians. The Christian "reception" of Hellenistic categories was not just a servile absorption of an undigested heathen heritage. Rather it was a conversion of the Hellenic mind itself. Everything was trans-valuated thereby. And having been converted, the Hellenic mind was fertilized for a new and Christian development. "Hellenistic categories" were in fact no greater limitations for Christian thought than was the Hebrew mind under the old dispensation.

Hellenism means philosophy. We have to distinguish carefully between philosophies and Philosophy. Clement of Alexandria was very strict about that. For him, Greek philosophy was a preparation of the Gospel, as a whole. But all the particular systems were only unsuccessful attempts to apprehend the general providential guidance. All of them are antiquated since the heavenly Master came in person to guide His people into the full Truth. For Clement, no less than for Tertullian, Athens is of no more value since the divine light shone from Jerusalem. But Philosophy has not been done away with. It has rather been given a new purpose. Ancient philosophers may have erred and have erred most dangerously indeed. Yet Christians must be philosophers themselves. For Philosophy means simply the vocation of the human mind to apprehend the ultimate Truth, now revealed and consummated in the incarnate Word. No particular philosophical system was ever adopted or authorized in the early Church. The Fathers were rather eclectic. They attempted a new philosophical synthesis on the basis of the revelation. Certainly, they linked the divine message they had to deliver with the aspirations of the Hellenic mind. They vindicated the right of the human mind to ask questions. But it was the revealed truth they were interpreting and commending. Individual writers may have gone too far; some of them went astray. One would naturally think here of Origen or of Pseudo-Dionysius. But on the whole the balance was kept. The new and Christian mind emerges from this philosophical quest. Modern scholars fervently hunt for the alien accretions in the patristic doctrine. Unfortunately, they so often miss just the kernel, the very system of this new Philosophy, which is Christian Dogmatics.

Medieval Scholasticism was perhaps overburdened with unreformed philosophy. Yet what was repudiated in the Reformation was Philosophy itself. Away from philosophy and back to the Bible, as if they were radically irreconcilable. This was the main idea of the early Reformers. What was to be eliminated was just the philosophical quest, the philosophical mentality itself. This proved to be impossible. And in the second generation, even the Aristotelian scholasticism was partly restored. Protestant theology on the continent was in the seventeenth century no less scholastic than the Counter-Reformation itself. But the true metaphysical spirit was lost. The breakaway from the patristic tradition in modern theology was motivated simply by a deep distrust of philosophy, by a desire to eliminate metaphysics from Christian doctrine. Morals and psychology were introduced instead. The metaphysical doctrine of man was reduced to a psychology. The immortality of the soul was overemphasized to such an extent as to miss the mortality of man, and the tragedy of human death was underestimated.

Christology was first affected by this deformation of the Christian doctrine of man. Christology was, as it were, "reduced." And it is obvious that no coherent doctrine of the atonement can ever be built except on a sound Christological basis. This "reduced Christology" (the phrase is Dr Sanday's) inevitably produces moralism and psychologism in soteriology. The basic doctrine of the hypostatical union seemed to be too metaphysical, and so was often practically neglected, sometimes plainly denied. But even in the better-balanced conceptions, the problem of salvation was dangerously moralized. This applies to the penal theory of the atonement also. The attempt was made in that theory to reconcile justice and love, divine majesty and human perversion, etc. But the ontology of salvation was almost overlooked. This also applied to the modern "kenotic" and moralistic conceptions. Strangely enough, these modern theories are much more abstract than the patristic metaphysics. They deal simply with general ideas. Sin and divine anger, nothingness and perfection, even justice and mercy, all these contrasts are very abstract indeed, and they are dealt with so often in the most dialectical manner. The crucifixion itself is so often interpreted less as a crucial event in time, than as a kind of symbol, which had to express the ultimate condemnation of sin by the divine righteousness. One thinks much more of the redemption than of the redeemer. Criticism is not within the scope of the present essay. A positive reconstruction of the original patristic doctrine is attempted instead. Possibly that is the best way of criticism.

One can find a fair presentation of the history of the patristic doctrine in J. Riviere's *The Dogma of Redemption* or in Prof. Grensted's *Short History of the Doctrine of the Atonement*, or elsewhere. My aim here is simply to introduce the reader to the common spirit of patristic theology, and to attempt a systematic reconstruction of the doctrine in the same spirit. In a brief essay it has hardly been possible to bring in all the available patristic references. I trust, however, that the selection I give here is at least fairly representative.

One special point must be stressed here. The patristic doctrine of the atonement was incorporated into the liturgy. Numerous quotations are given in this book from the liturgical sources, and it would be very easy to make many more to prove that we have here not only some private speculations or *theologoumena*, but the common mind of the worshipping Church. One can best be initiated into the spirit of the Fathers by attending the offices of the Eastern Church, especially in Lent and up to Trinity Sunday. Most of the hymns and collects used belong to the patristic epoch. The *lex credendi*, as presented in the patristic writings, is corroborated by the *lex orandi*. And again, this is the witness, not merely of the Eastern Church alone, but rather of the undivided Church of old, of the Church of the Fathers. One can compare it with the testimony of the early Latin Church, as exhibited by St Augustine or St Leo in his glorious liturgical sermons. And on the whole, one can describe the patristic doctrine of the atonement as a *liturgical* or *sacramental* theory, in contrast with any others—juridical, moralistic, or "political." In the sacramental practice and rites of the Church, the dogmatic teaching finds its fulfillment and expression, and the dogma is here again the living *kerygma* of salvation.

This book is an enlarged reproduction of a short course of lectures, delivered for the University of London, in November 1936 by the kind invitation of the University authorities. It is my pleasant duty to acknowledge here my deep gratitude to the Board of Theological Studies of the University for the privilege of lecturing at the University as well as for a generous grant toward the publication of the present volume. I have to thank particularly the Rev. Professor H. Maurice Relton, D.D., who presided over the first of my course of lectures. I lectured on the same subject at the Bishop's Hostel, Lincoln, and I have to thank the Rt. Rev. the Bishop of Jarrow, the then Warden, and the Rev. Chancellor J.H. Srawley, D.D., for their friendly encouragement and valuable advice, which was of great help in my research. I owe my thanks also to my friends, the Rev. C.A. Page, the Rev. Derwas J. Chitty, and the Rev. Denzil G.M. Patrick, for their kind assistance in the revision of this book, which had to be written in a language that is not my native tongue.

G.F.
"Les Serbiers"
Clarens (Vaud)
September 1939

✠

In Ligno Crucis
The church fathers' doctrine of redemption interpreted from the perspective of Eastern Orthodox theology[1]
Georges Florovsky, Paris[2]

Tᴀ HIS STUDY IS NOT A HISTORIC STUDY, nor should it be seen as a chapter in a dogmatic system. My purpose is much more limited. It is an attempt to present certain aspects of patristic thought, which are almost forgotten or neglected by modern theologians, even of the catholic tradition, and to show that by studying the Fathers it is possible to reacquire a firm basis for theological research. This study is a suggestion of what could be called a neo-patristic synthesis.

Agnus Dei. "And the Word became flesh" (John 1:14). This scriptural passage expresses the fullness of revelation. The incarnated Lord is both perfect God and a perfect human being. The incarnation reveals and realizes the full significance and highest meaning of human existence. He came down from heaven to save the world, to unite humanity with God for all eternity. In the incarnation human nature was assumed in an intimate and hypostatic union with the Godhead itself. In this elevation of human nature to an eternal union with divine life, the Fathers of the ancient church unanimously saw the essence of salvation, the foundation of the whole redemptive work of Christ. "That which is united with God is saved," says St Gregory Nazianzen. And that which was not united with the Godhead could not be saved. This was the main reason why he claimed against Apollinarius that the only-begotten Son received a complete human nature in the incarnation. This was the main theme in all ancient theology. This history of Christological dogma was determined by this basic idea: the incarnation of the Word as salvation.

---

[1]"In Lingo Crucis: kyrkofädernas lära om försoningen, tolkad från den grekisk-ortodoxa teologins synpunkt." *Svensk Teologisk Kvartalskrift* 23 (1947): 297–308. This translation into English is by David Heith-Stade, Lund University, Sweden. Included here with permission.

[2]Dr Florovsky, professor at the Eastern Orthodox Russian Academy in Paris, gave a lecture on this topic in Lund in the autumn of 1946. This article is a summary and translation from the English manuscript of this lecture (the manuscript corresponds to 100 printed pages), which was made by Dr Bengt Strömberg, Lund.

The incarnation of the Word was a revelation of life; Christ is the Word of Life. But the highpoint of the Gospel is the Cross; the death of the incarnated. Life was completely revealed in death. This is the paradoxical mystery of the Christian faith: life through death; life from the grave. We are born to a true eternal life only by our baptism into death and burial in Christ; we are reborn with Christ at the baptismal font. This is the unchanging law of the true life. "what you sow is not made alive unless it dies" (1 Cor 15:36).

Two things must be distinguished here: that Christ assumed human nature and that He took sin on Himself. He did not take the sin of the world on Himself in the incarnation. For sin is a voluntary act, not a natural necessity. He takes sin voluntarily; therefore, His work has a saving power as a free act of compassion and love.

The mystery of the Cross is unfathomable to reason. Christ explained that he *had* to die, not only that he would die. He had to die, but not in accordance with the law that reigns in this world where goodness and truth is persecuted. The death of Christ was voluntary. He chose to die. This choice did not mean that He passively let unrighteousness triumph. He wanted to die and He had to die in accordance with the law of truth and love. The crucifixion was a sacrifice. But the necessity of the sacrifice did not have its foundation in the conditions of this world but in in the divine love. The mystery of the Cross has its origin in eternity and is fulfilled in history.

The Church has never tried to give a rational definition of the mystery of the Cross. Biblical terms are the most adequate. Ethical and juridical views are only colorless anthropomorphisms. This also applies to the idea of sacrifice. The sacrifice of Christ cannot only be perceived as a sacrifice or victim, since then the necessity of death would be inexplicable. The whole life of the incarnated was an uninterrupted sacrifice. Why would this life not be enough to conquer death? Christ was not a passive victim but a conqueror even in the greatest humiliation. And He knew that this humiliation not only meant long-suffering and obedience, but that it was the way of glory and final victory.

The concept *iustitia vindicativa* does not reveal the inner meaning of the sacrifice of the Cross. The mystery of the Cross cannot be adequately expressed in terms such as satisfaction, retribution, or ransom. If the value of the death of Christ was increased infinitely because of His divinity, so was His whole life. All His acts have an infinite value as acts of the incarnated Word of God. And they superabundantly cover all the sins of mankind. And finally there is hardly any place for retributive justice in the death of Christ; for it was the suffering of the incarnated, of God's own Son, the suffering of an immaculate human nature, which had already been deified by being assumed into the hypostasis of the Word.

The *satisficatio vicaria* of the schoolmen is also not a useful idea. God does not seek the suffering of mankind. He grieves over suffering. The death of the incarnated can hardly mean that sin is destroyed if death itself is the wages of sin and death only exists in the sinful world. Does justice really keep back love and mercy, and was the crucifixion necessary to reveal God's forgiving love which otherwise would be precluded because of His vengeful justice?

Gens Mortalium. Humankind was created to live in God. It received immortality at its creation, but only as a possibility. This possibility was lost in the Fall. Mankind became mortal. It was in one sense created mortal, but it was in a condition to escape death if it held on to God and His original gifts. It was placed between life and death and had a choice. The Fall was already a kind of death, an exclusion from the only source of life and immortality, a loss of the life-giving Spirit. Human death entered the world through sin. Separated from God, human nature loses its hold and becomes unstable. The union of soul and body becomes precarious. The body is turned into the prison of the soul. Physical death becomes unavoidable. Mankind is created from nothing and, during its existence, risks plunging into an abyss of nothingness.

The Christian experience views death as a metaphysical catastrophe. Death is not a normal end to human existence. God did not create death. He created humanity for incorruptibility. Human death is the wages of sin. What does it mean for a human person to die? It is apparently the body that dies, since only the body is mortal. We speak of the "immortal" soul. The issue of death is first and foremost an issue of the human body. Christianity does not only preach the life of the immortal soul, but also the resurrection of the body. Human death becomes a cosmic catastrophe. Nature loses its immortal center in the dying human person and dies itself in the human person. The human person is a kind of "microcosm." All kinds of life exist in him. Only through and in the human person will the whole world come into a relationship with God. The fall of humanity alienated the whole creation from God. It destroyed the cosmic harmony. Through the Fall, humanity became subject to the course of nature. This ought not to have happened. In the life of animals death is an expression of the power of procreation rather than of frailty. Through the fall of humanity, death also receives in nature an evil and tragic meaning. To the animals death means only the end of individual existence. Among humans death strikes at the personality, and personality is something more than mere individuality. The body is dissolved and subject to death because of sin. But the whole human person dies. The human person is composed of body and soul; therefore, the separation of body and soul means that the human person ceases to exist as a human person. The image of God fades. Death reveals that the human person, this creature made by God, is only a body. The fear of death reveals a deep metaphysical anguish and not only a sinful attachment to earthly things. The Fathers saw in the union of soul and body an analogy to the indivisible unity of the two natures in the hypostasis of Christ, which is one. In death the unity is destroyed. The fear of death is only averted through the hope of resurrection and eternal life.

Death does not only mean that sin is revealed; it is also an anticipation of resurrection. God does not only punish fallen human nature by death, but also purifies and heals it. The human person breaks in death like pottery, and the body dissolves again to ashes in order that, purified from the acquired impurity, he may be restored to the normal form through the resurrection. Death is, consequently, not something evil but a blessing. Death contains in itself the possibility of resurrection. The destiny of humankind can only be realized in the general resurrection. But only the resurrection of the Lord raised human nature and makes the general resurrection possible.

Redemption is, above all, the salvation from death and destruction, a restoration of the original unity and stability of human nature. But it is only possible to restore the unity in human nature by restoring the communion between humanity and God. The resurrection is only possible in God. Christ is the resurrection and the life. The way to and hope of resurrection was revealed in the incarnation. Humanity sinned but also fell into corruptibility; therefore, the Word of God became a human person and received our body. Death had been implanted in the body; therefore, life had to be implanted again in order to save it from corruptibility and clothe it with life. Else it would not be able to be resurrected.

The decisive reason for the death of Christ is the mortality of mankind. Christ suffered death, but He conquered death and corruptibility and destroyed the power of death. In the death of Christ, death itself receives a new meaning.

Seminarium Mortuorum. Death is a catastrophe for humankind. This is a basic principle of Christian anthropology. The human person is both spirit and body. The body belongs organically to the unity of human existence. And this may have been the greatest new idea of the original Christian message. Greek thought has always had a certain antipathy toward the body. The body was a prison in which the fallen soul was contained. The Christian belief in the resurrection of the body meant for the Greeks that the prison would be eternal and the soul always imprisoned. Sin meant impurity, and the body was the seat of impurity. Evil comes from defilement, not from the straying of the will. Christianity brings a new view of the body. Docetism was rejected from the beginning as a most pernicious temptation. Platonism seeks only the purification of the soul, but Christianity also seeks the purification of the body. Platonism preaches the final separation of soul and body. Christianity preaches the final cosmic transfiguration. At this point Aristotle is closer to Christianity than Plato. The human being is, according to Aristotle, a completely earthly being. Aristotle denies personal immortality. What remains after death is not human, does not belong to the individual. It is a divine element, immortal and eternal. This weakness of Aristotle is also his strength. He truly understands the unity of human existence. The human being is for Aristotle primarily an individual, an organism, a living unity. Soul and body are not two distinct elements united with each other, but two aspects of the same concrete reality. In this way, Aristotle provided the Christian philosophers with the elements from which a true view of personality could be constructed. The divide between the impersonal and eternal intellect and the personal but mortal soul was bridged by the new consciousness of a spiritual personality. The idea of personality was a Christian contribution to philosophy.

The resurrection is not a repetition. The Christian doctrine of the general resurrection is not identical with the "eternal return" of Stoicism. The resurrection is the true renewal, explanation, and reformation of the whole creation. This constitutes a real philosophical difficulty. How can we think of this change in a way that allows the identity to remain? The ancient authors only assert the identity without attempting any philosophical explanation. Origen was the first who did. The body has its principle, *eidos* (form), which cannot be destroyed in death. *Eidos* is *principium inividuationis* (principle of individuation). As indestructible, *eidos* also becomes *principium surgendi* (principle of resurrection). Regardless of the particles from which the resurrected body is formed, the *eidos* thus guarantees the identity. St Methodius of Olympus criticizes Origen's idea of *eidos*. Can the form remain if the body ceases to exist? In any case the identity of form is not a guarantee of the personal identity if the whole material substratum is something else. St Methodius thinks rather that the form is the same as the external shape of the body and not, as Origen, the internal life force; therefore, his critique of Origen is not to the point. But the tendency of Methodius to claim the unity of the human person is valuable. St Gregory of Nyssa tries to unite the views of Origen and Methodius. After the dissolution of the body the particles retain certain signs of the former connection with the soul. And even in each soul there are signs of the connection with the body. Because of these signs, the body is able to recognize its own corporal elements on the day of resurrection. The identity is safeguarded. It is the same human person who is resurrected.

The concept of identity has a meaning in Christian philosophy different from the Greek. In the latter it is a question of timeless identity, in the former of identity with a life, which has been experienced and lived. The perception of time is different in both cases. Greek philosophy does not know the transition from time to eternity. The temporal is *eo ipso* (by that very fact) ephemeral. What is born must die. Only that which is unborn, without origin, remains. A future immortality is, therefore, always united in Greek thought with an eternal pre-existence. Everything that is worthy of existence exists in unchangeable static timelessness, and nothing can be added to its perfection. Time is symbolized in Greek philosophy by a circle. It is a rotation without end. There is no real history. The perception of time changes radically with Christianity. Time has a beginning and an end. It is unique and will never return. The final limit of time is the general resurrection. The temporal order is a creative process wherein that which has been created from nothing by divine will proceeds to its final perfection, on the last day, when the divine purpose will be fulfilled. And the center of history is the incarnation and the incarnated Lord's victory over death and sin. St Augustine expresses the change made by Christianity in his famous statement: "*Viam rectam sequentes, quae nobis est Christus, eo duce ac salvatore, a vano et inepto impiorum circuitu iter fidei mentemque avertamus*" (Following the straight way, which for us is Christ, with Him as both leader and savior, let us turn the path of faith and our mind away from the futile and senseless circle of the impious; *City of God* 12.21).

Triduum Mortis. The Letter to the Hebrews describes the Lord's work of salvation as the ministry of a high priest. The sacrifice of Christ began on earth and was fulfilled in heaven, where Christ as the eternal high priest offers and still offers us to God. The death of Christ on the cross is a sacrifice. The efficacious power of the sacrifice is love. But this love is not only compassion with the fallen. The sacrifice means that Christ gives Himself not only for the sins of the world but also for our glorification. He sacrifices Himself not only for sinful humanity, but also for the church in order to make her holy, glorious, and pure (cf. Eph 5:25).

The death on the Cross was not efficacious because it was the death of an innocent man, but because it was the death of the incarnated Lord. It was not a human being who died on the cross but God. But God died in His own humanity. He was Himself the resurrection and life. His death was human, but it took place in the hypostasis of the incarnated Word; therefore, it led to resurrection.

In Luke 12:50 the Lord speaks of the baptism with which He has to be baptized. This baptism is the death on the cross. This is a baptism of blood, a purification of human nature in the shedding of the sacrificial blood of the Lamb and foremost a purification of the body. Not only sin is washed away, but also human weakness and mortality itself. It is a purification in order to prepare for the coming resurrection. It is a purification of the whole human nature in the firstborn, in the person of "the second Adam." This is the baptism of blood of the whole Church. The death on the cross is also a purification of the whole world, a baptism of blood of the whole creation. The whole of creation participates in a mystical way in the suffering unto death of the incarnated Lord.

The death on the cross is a sacrament. It has a sacramental and liturgical meaning, which is revealed at the Last Supper. The Eucharist is the sacrament of crucifixion, the broken body and the shed blood. It is also the sacrament of transfiguration, the mystical and sacramental "change" of the flesh into the glorifying spiritual nourishment.

The death of Christ on the cross was a real death. But it was not like our death because it was the death of the Lord, of the incarnated Word, a death in the indivisible hypostasis of the Word, which had become a human being. And when the Lord voluntarily took on Himself the sins of the world, this did not mean that He had to die. In His saving love, He decided to die. The body and soul became definitely separated in this death. But the one hypostasis of the incarnated Word was not divided. The "hypostatic union" was neither broken nor destroyed. In other words, although the soul and body were separated in death, they nevertheless remained united through the divinity of the Word. This does not change the ontological character of death but its meaning. The death of Christ was a "death without corruption" and therefore corruptibility and death were conquered in it and resurrection began in it.

There are two aspects of the mystery of the Cross. It is both a mystery of sorrow and joy, of disgrace and glory. The Church guards against every docetistic devaluation of the reality and fullness of Christ's suffering. On the other hand, she also guards against the opposite exaggeration, against kenotic overemphasis. The death of Christ is by itself a victory over death not only because it is followed and crowned with the resurrection, for this only reveals and manifests the victory of the Cross. The power of the resurrection is the same as the "power of the Cross."

"The three days of death" (*triduum mortis*) are the mystical days of resurrection. The Lord rests in the grave with His body, and His body is not abandoned by His divinity. The body of the Lord did not suffer corruptibility, since it remained in the womb of life itself, in the hypostasis of the Word. The soul of Christ descends into hell also without being separated from the divinity. The descent into hell means primarily an intrusion into the kingdom of death, mortality, and corruptibility. And in this sense hell is synonymous with death. The Lord descended into hell as the victor, *Christus Victor*, the master of life. He descended in His glory, not in His humiliation. The descent into hell is the resurrection of the "whole Adam." Christ destroys death. The resurrection triumphs.

Totus Christus, caput et corpus. The death of the Saviour revealed that death held no power over him. The Lord was mortal in respect of His complete human nature; for even in the original nature there was a *potentia mortis* (capacity of death). The Lord died, but death could not keep Him. He was the eternal life, and through His death He destroyed death. His descent into hell, the kingdom of death, is the powerful revelation of life. By descending into hell, He gives life to death itself. And by the resurrection, the powerlessness of death is revealed. The reality of death is not repealed, but its powerlessness is revealed. In the death of the Lord, the power of the resurrection becomes apparent, which is concealed but intrinsic to every death. The parable of the wheat can be fully applied to His death. In the case of the body of the incarnated, the period between death and resurrection has been shortened. The seed grows to perfection in three days: *triduum mortis*. During this mystical *triduum mortis* the body of the Lord was transfigured, glorified, and clothed in power and light. The resurrection happened by the power of God, and by the same power the general resurrection will happen on the last day. In the resurrection the incarnation is perfected, a victorious revelation of life in the human nature. Immortality was grafted to humanity.

The resurrection of Christ was not only His victory over His own death but over death in general. In His resurrection the whole human nature is resurrected, but not so that all rise from the graves, for mankind still must die. But death has become powerless, and the whole human nature has received the ability to be resurrected.

We must distinguish between the healing of nature and of the will. Nature is healed and renewed with a certain coercion, the omnipotent and irresistible grace of God. We could speak of a "coercion of grace." This renewal will be realized and revealed in its full extent at the general resurrection, when everyone, both the righteous and the evil will be resurrected. No one can, as far as nature is concerned, escape the reign of Christ and be free from the irresistible force of the resurrection. But the human will cannot be healed in this irresistible way, for the will must be healed through voluntary repentance. The human will must turn itself to God. It must be a free and spontaneous response of love and worship. Only by this spontaneous and free effort does mankind enter eternal life, which is revealed in Jesus Christ. A spiritual rebirth can only take place in freedom, in obedience to love, by dedicating oneself to God. The way of life is the way of self-denial and sacrifice. We must die with Christ in His suffering and Cross in order to be able to live with Him. The Christian life begins with a new birth through water and the Spirit.

The symbolism of sacred baptism is rich. Baptism must be performed in the name of the Holy Trinity, and the invocation of the Trinity is unanimously seen as a necessary condition for the validity and efficacy of the sacrament. But the primary meaning of baptism is that we are clothed in Christ and incorporated into His Body. The invocation of the Trinity is necessary since it is impossible to come to know Christ outside the trinitarian faith, which recognizes that Jesus is the incarnated Lord, "one of the Holy Trinity" (Second Antiphon, Divine Liturgy of St John Chrysostom). But the symbolism of baptism is primarily concerned with the resurrection in Christ, a resurrection with Him and in Him to a new eternal life. In baptism the believers become limbs of Christ. And eternal life manifests itself in the spiritual rebirth of the faithful and is given and perfected in baptism, before it is perfected at the general resurrection. The union with the resurrected Lord is already the beginning of resurrection and eternal life. All will be resurrected but only for the faithful will the resurrection be a real resurrection to life. They will not come under judgment but pass from death to life.

The rite of initiation was not divided in the ancient church, but the three sacraments—baptism, confirmation, and Eucharist—were united. The sacraments are instituted in order to allow mankind to partake of the saving death of Christ and through it to receive the grace of His resurrection. The whole sacramental and devotional life of the church manifests and reflects the Cross and the resurrection in a diversity of symbols and rites. But this symbolism is realistic. The symbols not only remind us of something in the past, but they truly reveal and communicate the highest reality. This whole hieratic symbolism culminates in the exalted mystery of the altar. The Eucharist is the heart of the church, the sacrament of salvation in a special sense. The Eucharist is the Last Supper, celebrated again and again but never repeated. For every new celebration of the Eucharist not only represents, but is really the same mystical supper, which the Divine High Priest Himself celebrated for the first time. And the Lord himself is the real celebrant at every liturgy. The Last Supper was an offering of the sacrifice of the Cross, and this offering continues still. Christ still acts as the high priest in His Church. The mystery is the same. The sacrifice is one and the altar is one. And the priest is the same. It is the same lamb which is slain always and everywhere, the "Lamb of God who takes away the sin of the world" (John 1:29), the Lord Jesus. The Eucharist is not a sacrifice because Jesus is slain again, but because it is the same body and sacrificial blood that are really present at the altar and are sacrificed and offered. The altar is really the holy grave in which the Heavenly Master rests. And in the Eucharist the resurrecting power of Christ's death and its significance are completely revealed. The lamb is slain, the body is broken, the blood is shed, and still it is heavenly nourishment and "the medicine of immortality and antidote to death," to quote the famous words of St Ignatius (*Epistle to the Ephesians* 20:2). The Eucharist is a sacramental anticipation, a foretaste of the resurrection. The sacramental life of the faithful builds the Church. The new life in Christ is given to the limbs of His body through the sacraments. One may add: in the sacraments the incarnation is fulfilled—the final union of humankind with God in Christ.

☩

Redemption (Précis of a Planned Book)

Georges Florovsky

THE DOCTRINE OF REDEMPTION is the center of Christian theology, of which it is also the starting point. Indeed, the Son of God "came down from heaven for us men and for our salvation," as the redeemer of mankind (Nicene Creed). Whatever else may be said about the first "cause" of the incarnation (and at this point there is room for a variety of theological options), its immediate redemptive *purpose* is obvious. The main message of the Gospel is the message of salvation. We believe in Christ as in our saviour. This message presupposes that man is in need of redemption, that is, that he is in a predicament, or bad state. Thus, the doctrine of sin and the Fall is an immediate preamble to the doctrine of redemption. The theological interpretation of redemption depends upon the conception of sin. On the other hand, the doctrine of man's redemptive "restitution" is closely related to the general doctrine of man and to the conception of the ultimate creative design of God. Again, redemption is a manifestation of the divine concern about man, a manifestation of the divine love: "God so loved the world" (John 3:16). Of course, these presuppositions cannot be dealt with at full length in a treatise on redemption. Nor can they be simply referred to in advance, in a "preface," as it were. Actually, they constitute the perspective in which the doctrine of redemption must be presented. They must permeate the whole exposition. Moreover, we have to distinguish between "doctrine"—in the strict sense of the term—and "theology." Indeed, "doctrine" is a matter of faith, *credendum de fide* (something to be believed concerning the faith), and "theology" is a realm of *interpretation*, rational or spiritual, and there is here a certain room for freedom and for a variety of options, as difficult as it is to draw an exact line of demarcation. In any case, the treatise on redemption is inevitably a kind of *epitome* of the whole of Christian doctrine. It cannot be presented as a closed unit. For that reason, it is hardly possible to establish in advance a rigid outline of the treatise. It is difficult to say, in advance, how much of the "presuppositions" should be actually included in the exposition, and in what manner, and at what length. This can be discovered only in the process of actual composition. The same should be said of the "implications" of redemption.

No more than a tentative outline can be submitted in advance—open to revision and amplification.

Redemption is an *historic event*, as much as it is also an *eternal design*. It is a sovereign deed of God, but it is also an offer to man, and man's response in faith belongs to the very structure of the actual redemption. The world *has been redeemed*, once and forever, but it *is still being redeemed*, and *is to be redeemed*. Christ's coming is itself both an *accomplishment*, a consummation of the promise, and an *inauguration* of the New Covenant, of the New Humanity, of the "New Creation": Christ and His Body, the Church, cannot be separated. Indeed, the Church is precisely the "realm of redemption"—to be consummated at the end of times. The doctrine of redemption must be presented as the history of salvation, as *Heilsgeschichte*, in a wide perspective—from creation to consummation. On the one hand, we have to stress the unity of the biblical revelation, and this affects the very method to be used. *Novum testamentum in vetere latet, vetus testamentum in novo patet* .[1] In fact, basic categories of doctrinal interpretation are derived precisely from the Old Testament, although they appear in a new light in the context of the evangelical consummation: the Messiah, the Suffering Servant, the sacrifice, and the like. On the other hand, the full scope of the redemption will be disclosed only in the age to come, and, for that reason, the "realm of redemption" has intrinsically also an eschatological dimension.

There are several stages in the historic event itself:

1 "The Incarnation." It was the common assumption of the Fathers that the incarnation itself was already an act of redemption. The separated have been truly reunited, God and humanity. The early Christian soteriology was grounded in Christology. Moreover, the Christological dogma itself has been formulated precisely in the soteriological perspective and context. Any wrong shift in the Christological interpretation immediately affects the concept of redemption. The doctrine of redemption must be strictly and vigorously *Chalcedonian*. Yet, the dogma of Chalcedon is still variously interpreted by theologians, even within the strict limits of catholic faith and doctrine. It is enough to mention at this point the recent, and rather vigorous, controversy between the French Catholic theologians. Indeed, it is often no more than a problem of proper emphasis. The function of the two natures in Christ's redemptive act has still to be clarified. Moreover, the "incarnational aspect" of redemption is not seldom rather over-stressed. No doubt, there is no salvation except in the Incarnate One,

[1](The New Testament is hidden in the old, the Old Testament is opened up in the New; cf. St Augustine, *In heptateuchum* 2.73).

and by virtue of the incarnation. But incarnation is but the beginning of the redemptive event, of which it is the ground and presupposition. The climax of redemption is the cross and resurrection. *In hoc signo vinces* (In this sign you will conquer; cf. Rufinus, *Church History* 9.9)! Paradoxically, it appears that the Son of God "was made man" precisely in order to die and to destroy death by His own death and to rise. *Forma moriendi causa nascendi est* (the form of death is the cause of birth; Tertullian, *On the Flesh of Christ* 6.6). Taken in isolation, the doctrine of the Incarnation does not provide an adequate foundation for the catholic doctrine of redemption.

2 "The Life and the Historic Ministry of Christ." There are two correlated aspects. Christ's life itself—the life of the Suffering Servant, in lowliness and humiliation—sets a new pattern and a new norm. It is the pattern of the new Kingdom. In this sense, an *imitatio Christi* (imitation of Christ) is required and it has a redemptive significance. Actually, there is more than a pattern or just an example to be followed. Christians are summoned not only to "follow" Christ, but to be *in Christo*. Gross misinterpretations of the mystery of redemption were due, in the ancient times and even more in the present, to the disproportionate emphasis on the concept of pattern or example (e.g. Pelagianism, Abelard). On the other hand, Christ was the Teacher, and indeed, the only teacher. The evangelical pattern of life, as delineated in His parables and in the Sermon on the Mount, belonged to the very structure of His redemptive ministry. All events of Christ's life had a redemptive significance, including the Temptation, the Agony in the Garden, and also the miracles, which were the sign of the Kingdom. But the climax of His life was His death.

3 "The Death of Christ on the Cross." Again, there are two aspects: suffering and death itself. Very often the main stress is put, in theological interpretation, on the former, and the latter is somehow underestimated. In the theology of the Fathers, however, the death of Christ was regarded, in full conformity to the Scriptures, as His supreme redemptive victory; the Crucified was *Christus Victor*. This interpretation, which was also the basis of ancient sacramental theology, was grounded in the distinctive "theology of death," according to the Pauline concept of death as the "ultimate enemy" (1 Cor 15:26). The Life shines from the tomb. The two dimensions intersect and overlap: *status humilitationis* and *status gloriae* (condition of humiliation and condition of glory), so that *theologia crucis* (theology of the Cross) itself appears to be a *theologia gloriae* (theology of glory). In this connection, special attention must be given to the creedal

concept of *descensus* (descent). The Crucifixion is a sacrifice inaugurating the New Covenant, "in His blood." The cross itself is the new "tree of life." At this point, various, and often discordant, theological theories must be carefully analyzed and evaluated.

4 "The Resurrection, Ascension, and the Heavenly Glory." It is the consummation of the redemption and a token of general resurrection, an inauguration of the new Kingdom.

5 "The Realm of Redemption: The Church and the Sacraments." Sacraments as participation in the redemptive deed of Christ: Baptism and Eucharist.

6 "The Consummation."

At the present, it is difficult to give a detailed outline of the last sections. The basic emphasis will be Christological, in the light of the doctrine of *totus Christus* (the whole Christ; Augustine, *Expositions on the Psalms* 74.4).

The main purpose of the present tentative outline is to distinguish clearly the stages of Christ's redemptive deed and to clarify their interdependence. The scheme is systematic. But the method is exegetical, with due attention to the voice of Tradition.

There are a number of special issues, which may be treated in appendices:

A "Cur Deus homo?" What is the relation between the eternal decree of creation and the redemptive history? This point is of special importance in the contemporary theological situation. I have in view, in particular, the new trend in theology inaugurated recently by P. Teilhard de Chardin for which I have personally no sympathy. The problem is real, but the solution is wrong.

B "The Kenosis." It is a specific topic in Christology highly relevant for the interpretation of the redemptive aspect of the Incarnation.

C "Man's mortality as the 'wages of sin.' The 'Redemption of the Body.'"

D "Martyrdom as participation in Christ's Sacrifice."

E "The Last Supper and Calvary (with reference to *Mysterium Fidei* of P. M. de la Taille)."

F "Apocatastasis and Eternal Damnation."

I do not believe it would be profitable to go into further detail for the moment. Concrete issues will arise in the process of research and actual writing.

G.F.

☩

The Stumbling-Block[1]
Georges Florovsky

"For I decided to know nothing among you except Jesus Christ, and him crucified."

—1 Cor 2:2

THE MYSTERY OF THE CROSS was for the great apostle the heart of the gospel. It was the revelation of God's glory and love. It was the crucial message of Christian faith. Now Paul was fully aware that this message was for the outsiders an offense, a scandal, a stumbling block. Unto the Jews it was a stumbling block, indeed. Unto the Greeks, or the gentiles, it was a nonsense, a foolishness (1 Cor 1:23). Paul knew but too well the whole strength of this offense. He came himself to faith through a crisis. At first he violently resisted the message of Christ, and was for a time in the camp of persecutors. "For you have heard of my former life in Judaism, how I persecuted the church of God violently and tried to destroy it" (Gal 1:13). He knew by his own experience, how difficult it was for many to accept and to comprehend the mystery of Christ, crucified and risen. It was difficult for him, as it was difficult for so many others, precisely because he was "so extremely . . . zealous for the traditions" of his elders (Gal 1:14).

Indeed, the apostolic preaching contradicted sharply the current expectations of the Jews, and it did not appeal to the sophisticated wise of the heathen. The Jews failed to recognize the promised and expected Messiah, the "one who should have come," in Jesus of Nazareth. Their reasons were obvious. Their resistance and their hesitations are so plainly described in the Gospel narratives. Most of them expected the coming of a mighty prince who would restore the external strength and splendor of the Jewish kingdom, liberate Israel from the foreign yoke and power of Rome, and "reign over the house of Jacob forever" (Luke 1:33).

[1]Originally published in Alton M. Motter, ed., *Preaching the Passion: Twenty-Four Outstanding Sermons for the Lenten Season* (Philadelphia, PA: Fortress Press, 1963), 26–35. Reprinted here with permission.

Indeed, people were often moved by Jesus' preaching, and even more by His miracles. They listened to Him readily and with expectation. On occasion they were even ready to "take him by force and make him king" (John 6:15). But Jesus persistently declined any political involvement. He was a King, and He preached the coming of a kingdom. But this kingdom of God was "not of this world." Jesus was not concerned with the political liberation of Israel, while this liberation was probably the major dream of His contemporaries. He brought to men another freedom, the freedom from sin. He liberated men from another, from an internal bondage, the bondage of sin, not from external or political bondage. And this was a stumbling block. Some others at that time were expecting a celestial redeemer, coming on clouds, with a heavenly glory and escort. Jesus betrayed also this expectation. He came in "the form of a servant," humble, meek, lowly; He was born in poverty, and hardly had a place to lay His head. Finally, He was taken and crucified, was, as it were, defeated by the authorities of the state and of the synagogue.

Thus, the cherished hopes of the multitudes were belied and frustrated. As Paul says, "the Jews demand signs" (1 Cor 1:22), but our Lord refused to give such a sign: "an evil and adulterous generation seeks for a sign; but no sign shall be given to it, except the sign of the prophet Jonah" (Matt 12:39). The only messianic sign which Jesus gave was precisely His Cross, His death, His stay among the dead for three days, as Jonah was three days in the whale's belly. Again, this sign was rather a challenge and a stumbling block. Why should the anointed of the Lord have suffered so shamefully, so helplessly, and so conspicuously, instead of manifesting His might, and splendor, and glory? This passed all knowledge and understanding. And it was for that reason that but a few believed in Him, and even those who did acknowledge Christ during His earthly ministry were so uncertain and hesitant, and were confounded when He was betrayed. "Then all the disciples forsook him and fled" (Matt. 26:56). They failed to recognize in the humiliated Christ, in the Suffering Servant, the promised deliverer and Messiah. The faith of the disciples was restored and quickened only by the risen Lord.

Paul knew but too well all these doubts and temptations of frail men. He was himself converted by a personal intervention of the Lord. He was surprised and overtaken by an invincible miracle, in a mysterious encounter with Jesus whom he was persecuting. And once converted, Paul could never forget the cost of faith. He was conscious of all obstacles which may impede belief. In his preaching he never compromised, he never tried to make his message easy for his flock, not for them whom he was to evangelize. Just the opposite: he stressed in his preaching precisely that stumbling-block. The Crucified One was the Lord, and His Lordship was revealed and assured precisely in His suffering and death. Indeed, the ultimate message of Paul was the gospel of resurrection.

Writing to the church in Corinth, Paul begins with the "foolishness" of God, with the "scandal" of the Cross, and ends with the mystery of the resurrection. But Christ's resurrection was the fruit of the Cross. This is the basic pattern of Christian life: one has to die with Christ, to share in His death in order to rise with Him and to share in the new life, which as it were, shines from the tomb of the crucified.

Of course, there was nothing specifically "Pauline" in this preaching of the Cross. It was, indeed, the common faith of the whole church. Paul used to stress emphatically that this was tradition, and not his peculiar interpretation. "For I delivered to you as of first importance what I also received, that Christ died for our sins in accordance with the Scriptures" (1 Cor 15:3). But probably Paul was the greatest preacher of this astounding and stumbling "good news" because his own faith went through such a hectic trial and had all the heat of radical conversion: from "breathing threats and murder against the disciples of the Lord" (Acts 9:1) to triumphant insight into the glory of the crucified. Nothing else, save Jesus, and Him crucified!

"According to the Scriptures" . . . Indeed, one could have gathered from the Scriptures enough evidence to identify Jesus as deliverer, but even the disciples did not "know" the Scriptures. It was the risen Lord Himself who had opened their minds to understand what had been written of Him in the Law, in the Psalms, and in the Prophets. Their hearts also had to be quickened. Strangely enough, most of the contemporaries of Jesus would never remember the glorious prophecy of Isaiah about the Suffering Servant, which came to be regarded in the Church as a most conspicuous anticipation of the victory of the Cross. They would not connect this prophecy of doom and grief with the promise of deliverance, recovery, and restoration. And yet, there was, in this magnificent vision, a paradoxical merger of sorrow and exaltation. "My servant . . . shall be exalted and lifted up, and shall be very high" (Isa 52:13). But he will be also a "man of sorrows, and acquainted with grief" (53:3). Both despised and exalted: this is precisely the mystery of Jesus! It seems that Jesus Himself used to interpret His mission precisely in the terms of this prophetic vision. In any case, the prophecy of Isaiah came to be interpreted in this way quite early in the church. It was in the terms of this prophecy that Philip would preach Jesus unto the man of Ethiopia (Acts 8:32ff.). Indeed, it was a prophecy of deliverance, an announcement of the redeeming sacrifice: it was "with his stripes" that men were to be healed (Isa 53:5).

This vision of the "man of sorrows," and the belief in the redeeming sacrifice, formed the deepest conviction of Paul. The whole perspective had been changed. Salvation had come, not in a spectacular and triumphant manner, but through the Cross. This was Paul's message to the churches: "But God shows his love for us in that while we were yet sinners Christ died for us" (Rom. 5:8). The death of Christ is a sign and a token of divine love! By the blood of His Cross all things were reconciled to Himself (Col. 1:20). His Cross is the instrument and the sign of universal peace and reconciliation! For that reason the preaching of the Cross was a stumbling-block for many in the ages past, and is still a stumbling-block in our own time. Only now we prefer to speak of a "paradox."

The mystery of the Cross is beyond our rational comprehension. It seems to be a foolishness to the wise of this world. The whole life of Christ was one great act of love and mercy. The whole of it was illuminated by the eternal radiance of His loving-kindness. But the act of salvation was consummated and completed on Calvary, not on Mount Tabor.

And the Cross of Jesus, His "exodus," was foretold even on Tabor (Luke 9:31). Christ came not only that He might teach with authority and disclose to people the name of the Father, not only that He might display and accomplish works of mercy. He came precisely to suffer and to die. More than once He witnessed to this before the perplexed and startled disciples. But even Peter could not stand this witness. "And Peter took him and began to rebuke him, saying, 'God forbid, Lord! This shall never happen to you.'" But Jesus reprimanded him sternly: "'. . . You are a hindrance to me; for you are not on the side of God, but of men'" (Matt. 16:22–23). The human mind cannot comprehend the mind of God!

Moreover, His death was in no sense an accident. It was preordained in God's design of salvation. He had to die. He suffered and died, not because He could not escape it, but because He chose to do so. He had the "authority" to lay down His life (John 10:18). He chose so, not merely in the sense that He permitted the rage of sin and unrighteousness to be vented on Himself. He not only permitted but willed it. He had to die according to the law of divine wisdom and love. In no way was the crucifixion a kind of passive suicide, or a simple murder. It was a sacrifice and an oblation. It was not so much a necessity of this world. Rather, it was a constraint of the divine love. The mystery of the Cross begins in eternity. Hence, Christ is spoken of in the Scriptures as the Lamb who was "destined before the foundation of the world" (1 Pet 1:20). Or, in the phrase of a great preacher of last century, "the Cross of Jesus, composed of the enmity of the Jews and the violence of the Gentiles, was but the earthly image and shadow of the heavenly Cross of love" (Philaret, Metropolitan of Moscow, 1816).

This divine necessity of Christ's death passes all understanding, indeed; and the church has never attempted any rational solution of this supreme mystery. Scriptural terms have appeared, and do still appear, to be the most adequate ones.

In the glorious Epistle to the Hebrews the redeeming work of Christ is depicted as the ministry of the high priest. Christ comes into the world to accomplish the will of God. Through the eternal Spirit He offers His own self to God, offers His blood for the remission of human sins, and this He accomplishes through His passion. By His blood, as the blood of the New Covenant, He enters heaven and enters within the very Holy of Holies, behind the veil. This sacrificial offering begins on earth, but is consummated in heaven, where, as the eternal high priest, the "high priest of the good things to come," the mediator of the New Covenant, Christ presented and is still presenting us to God. In the blood of Jesus was revealed the new way, the way into that eternal Sabbath, when God rests from all His mighty deeds.

At this point we must beware of the legalistic misinterpretation of sacrifice. Sacrifice, indeed, is not just a surrender. It is, above all, dedication, or consecration to God. And the effective power of sacrifice is love: "as Christ loved us and gave himself up for us, a fragrant offering and sacrifice to God" (Eph 5:2). This love was not only sympathy, or compassion and mercy toward the fallen and heavy-laden. Christ gives Himself not only "for the remission of sins," but also for the glorification of the Church: to cleanse and hallow her, to make her holy, glorious and spotless. The power of a sacrificial offering is in its cleansing and hallowing effect.

The power of the sublime sacrifice of the Cross is in that the Cross itself is the path of glory. On the Cross the Son of man is glorified, and God is glorified in Him (John 13:31). The prayer of Christ as high priest was concerned precisely with the glory of the disciples: "the glory which thou has given me I have given to them" (John 17:22). Here is the fullness of the sacrifice. "Was it not necessary that the Christ should suffer these things and enter into his glory?" (Luke 24:26). In one of his great sermons, St John Chrysostom put it sharply: "today we keep the feast, for our Lord is nailed upon the Cross ... I call him King because I see Him crucified, for it is appropriate for a king to die for His subjects."

The mystery of the Cross is the mystery of the love divine. And for that reason the Cross is the seal of salvation. But the mystery is even deeper than that. The death of Christ is itself the resurrection. By His Cross He descended into that darkness of human death, which was the wages of sin and the prison of captive souls. And by the bliss of His divine glory He has destroyed the power of death, has abrogated death, and opened the new way of life and resurrection. He is Himself the resurrection and life. He rose from the dead because it was not possible for Him to be held by it (Acts 2:24).

But He did not rise alone. His resurrection is just the token of general resurrection, as Paul endeavored to explain in the same epistle to the Corinthian church. The power of the Cross, by which Christ has descended into the darkness of human existence, is the power of life, the power and the glory of resurrection. Thus, the sting of sin is taken away when the wages of sin, death, is abrogated.

For those, however, who do not believe, do not grasp the power of divine love, do not taste by faith the power of Christ, the stumbling-block remains, and the wisdom and the power of God may still seem to be but foolishness. But even Christians would sometimes require "a sign," in a Jewish manner, "or seek after wisdom," like the Gentiles. And the stumbling block of Christ's Cross may be strengthened by the superficial survey of Christian history, of the story and the destiny of the Church, which is Christ's Body. The Church still trods the path of her Lord, the path of lowliness and humiliation, of sorrow and tribulation, as Christ Himself has predicted: "In the world you have tribulation; but be of good cheer, I have overcome the world" (John 16:33).

The history of the church is also a stumbling block. It may seem to be a defeat. Was she victorious in her historic life? The Church corporately, and Christians individually, are still but suffering servants of the Lord, yea, of the crucified Lord, and the way of Christians in history was, is, and, according to Christ's own warning, will ever be "the way of the Cross." And it should be so: it is only this narrow path that leads into the Kingdom. The "humiliated Church" is as much a stumbling block as Christ's Cross itself. But it is in this way that the quickening of the world is being wrought by God. The message of Paul assumes a special reverence and poignancy in an age of crisis and trial, like ours.

The victory of the Cross can never by taken away. But it is not necessarily to be revealed or manifested in human splendor. The true deliverance is in that new life which is bestowed upon believers by the Spirit Paraclete, by which they are united with Christ and, in Him, with each other. It is this mystery of being in Christ, through the power of the Spirit, that Paul was so powerfully proclaiming both in his oral teaching and in his letter to the churches. He was a preacher of the Cross, but he was also a preacher of the church, being "the Body of Christ." "I, Paul, became a minister. Now I rejoice in my sufferings for your sake, and in my flesh I complete what is lacking in Christ's afflictions for the sake of his body, that is, the Church" (Col 1:23–24).

The destiny of man, and the whole of mankind, is decided indeed, not on battlefields, and not in the negotiations of "the wise." "Where is the wise man? Where is the scribe? Where is the debater of this age?" paraphrases Paul of the questions of Isaiah. They are in the inner chamber of human mind and heart, when one is brought face to face with the Lord Jesus, yea with the crucified redeemer of the world. The real stumbling block of human pride and impatience, of human vainglory and selfishness, is removed only by faith. The real stumbling block indeed is not Christ's lowliness and humiliation, but precisely the pride and foolishness of "the natural man," as Paul styles the unregenerate. In spite of his bonds and tribulations, Paul himself was always cheerful, full of joy, because he knew with an ultimate confidence of faith that the crucified was the Lord of glory, the Lord of all creation, to whom all power had been given on earth and in heaven, as a crown of his obedience.

Indeed, believers are given "a sign," which was refused to the Jews—even "the sign of the Cross." And "wisdom" is granted unto them also, which the Greeks sought in vain. For "to those who are called, both Jews and Greeks, Christ [is] the power of God and the wisdom of God" (1 Cor 1:24). Amen.

Contributors

Khaled Anatolios is Professor in the Department of Theology at Notre Dame University and serves as a priest in the Melkite Greek Catholic Church.

Matthew Baker (+2015) was adjunct professor in Theology at Hellenic College/Holy Cross Greek Orthodox School of Theology and received his Ph.D. posthumously from Fordham University. He was a priest in the Orthodox Church.

John Behr is Dean and Professor of Patristics at St Vladimir's Orthodox Theological Seminary, as well as Distinguished Lecturer in Patristics at Fordham University. He is an archpriest in the Orthodox Church.

Seraphim Danckaert is Director of Mission Advancement at St. Tikhon's Orthodox Theological Seminary and currently a Ph.D. candidate in theology at the Amsterdam Centre of Eastern Orthodox Theology, Vrije Universiteit Amsterdam. He is a reader in the Orthodox Church.

Nicholas Marinides is a postdoctoral research fellow in the Department of Theology at the University of Basel. He is a reader in the Orthodox Church.

John McGuckin is Ane Marie and Bent Emil Nielsen Professor in Late Antique and Byzantine Christian History at Union Theological Seminary and also Professor of Byzantine Christian Studies at Columbia University. He is an archpriest in the Orthodox Church.

Marcus Plested is Associate Professor in the Department of Theology at Marquette University.

Irenei Steenberg is Dean of Saints Cyril & Athanasius of Alexandria Institute for Orthodox Studies and a visiting professor at Santa Clara University. He is an archimandrite in the Orthodox Church.

Alexis Torrance is Assistant Professor and the Archbishop Demetrios College Chair of Byzantine Theology at Notre Dame University. He is a reader in the Orthodox Church.